D0914832

MOVE

How Decisive Leaders
Execute Strategy
DESPITE
Obstacles, Setbacks, & Stalls

MOVE

PATTY AZZARELLO

WILEY

Cover image: © TOMOGRAF/GETTY IMAGES, INC.
Cover design: Wiley

Copyright © 2017 by John Wiley & Sons, Inc. All rights reserved.

Published by John Wiley & Sons, Inc., Hoboken, New Jersey.
Published simultaneously in Canada.

No part of this publication may be reproduced, stored in a retrieval system, or transmitted in any form or by any means, electronic, mechanical, photocopying, recording, scanning, or otherwise, except as permitted under Section 107 or 108 of the 1976 United States Copyright Act, without either the prior written permission of the Publisher, or authorization through payment of the appropriate per-copy fee to the Copyright Clearance Center, 222 Rosewood Drive, Danvers, MA 01923, (978) 750-8400, fax (978) 646-8600, or on the web at www.copyright.com. Requests to the Publisher for permission should be addressed to the Permissions Department, John Wiley & Sons, Inc., 111 River Street, Hoboken, NJ 07030, (201) 748-6011, fax (201) 748-6008, or online at www.wiley.com/go/permissions.

Limit of Liability/Disclaimer of Warranty: While the publisher and author have used their best efforts in preparing this book, they make no representations or warranties with respect to the accuracy or completeness of the contents of this book and specifically disclaim any implied warranties of merchantability or fitness for a particular purpose. No warranty may be created or extended by sales representatives or written sales materials. The advice and strategies contained herein may not be suitable for your situation. You should consult with a professional where appropriate. Neither the publisher nor the author shall be liable for damages arising herefrom.

For general information about our other products and services, please contact our Customer Care Department within the United States at (800) 762-2974, outside the United States at (317) 572-3993 or fax (317) 572-4002.

Wiley publishes in a variety of print and electronic formats and by print-on-demand. Some material included with standard print versions of this book may not be included in e-books or in print-on-demand. If this book refers to media such as a CD or DVD that is not included in the version you purchased, you may download this material at http://booksupport.wiley.com. For more information about Wiley products, visit www.wiley.com.

Library of Congress Cataloging-in-Publication Data:

Names: Azzarello, Patty, author.
Title: Move : how decisive leaders execute strategy despite obstacles,
    setbacks, and stalls / Patty Azzarello.
Description: Hoboken, New Jersey : John Wiley & Sons, Inc., [2017] | Includes index.
Identifiers: LCCN 2016044306 | ISBN 9781119348375 (cloth) | ISBN 9781119348368 (epub)
    | ISBN 9781119348405 (ePDF)
Subjects: LCSH: Strategic planning. | Organizational behavior. | Leadership.
Classification: LCC HD30.28 .A994 2017 | DDC 658.4/092–dc23 LC record available at https://
    lccn.loc.gov/2016044306

Printed in the United States of America

10 9 8 7 6 5 4 3 2 1

To Al and Jim

(In order of appearance)

CONTENTS

INTRODUCTION

Why Great Strategies and Change Initiatives Fail

A while back I was asked to participate in one of those executive leadership programs where you go off-site with your peers and role-play a business simulation over the course of a couple of days.

You found yourself in charge of a fictional business, needing to make smart decisions, trade-offs, and investments to grow your revenue and profits in competition with your peers and their pretend businesses.

One of the tools you had in this simulation was the ability to make investments in various predefined "initiatives." These initiatives were things like "manager training," "supply chain cost reduction," or "accelerating product development."

Investing in an initiative would result in an advantage, like extra profit from cost reductions or shorter time to market. You couldn't just apply these initiatives. Just like in the real world, if you wanted to invest in an initiative, you needed to find the money to fund it from somewhere else in the business. You could either make a short-term profit trade-off, or take investment from another part of the operation to fund the initiative.

But unlike the real world, all you needed to do was to choose an initiative and fund it—and then your business gained the advantage in the simulation. You simply wrote the check and collected the benefit. Just like that. Every time.

One of the most senior executives joked, "The great thing about these initiatives is that they actually work! In our world, we just spend the money on the initiative, and then it doesn't help. I wish our initiatives worked this well."

Everyone laughed.

Isn't that awful? That we can all so easily relate to spending money on strategic initiatives that don't work? Why do we keep doing this?

STRATEGY WITHOUT EXECUTION = TALKING

At the heart of every execution problem is the fact that there are not enough people doing what the business needs to move forward.

Whether we are talking about transformation, specific strategic initiatives, or overall business strategy, I frequently observe that execution stalls because of some particular, common, and chronic challenges—systemic issues that occur in all organizations, which leaders often just accept as an unchangeable part of the environment.

One of the challenges is being too busy. You can't get to be a $1B organization if you are too busy being a $200M organization. When short-term pressures regularly take priority over doing more strategic stuff, you end up burning all your time and resources reacting to issues and opportunities in an ad hoc manner, instead of making progress on the strategic work that will enable you to scale. New initiatives require new work. People (at all levels) are just too busy and distracted to get traction on or even start doing the new thing. It's not that your strategy is wrong or the initiative wouldn't help; it's that it doesn't get done because no one has time to do it.

Mid-Level Manager Stall

If you talk to the executives, they often cite frustration with mid-level managers and directors who are "not strategic enough," because they do not personally make the decisions and trade-offs necessary to actually get the new work done at their level and below. They keep waiting for direction from above.

Decision Stall

If you talk to the mid-level managers, they often cite that execs fail to provide enough clarity—there are persistent debates and unanswered questions that keep people waiting vs. doing. Also, lack of clarity causes an automatic lack of alignment that results in skepticism, weak support, or passive-aggressive tendencies in the ranks.

Resource Stall

Agreements about what should be started (and what should be stopped) are not clear or not even attempted. Resources stay attached, often fiercely so, to the current way of doing things—so it's virtually impossible to do different or new stuff.

Organizational Angst

There is no such thing as a perfect organization, but there are also some fatal flaws that will prevent forward progress. When you have the wrong people in key roles or a structure that is competing against itself, you will stall. Or when you have groups or programs that are just not functioning properly, you burn huge amounts of time and energy recovering from work that should have been done better or differently or faster.

WHY I WROTE *MOVE*

I personally find it very frustrating when organizations fail to progress, and I want to help.

There are answers to these chronic, systemic issues that stall forward progress—practical answers and doable things. Strategic investments actually can pay off. But the organizations that make their strategy successful do some specific things on purpose to accomplish it.

I always seemed to have a knack for stepping into stalled organizations and getting them moving forward or turning them around. As a CEO and general manager, I have always had an ability for getting teams focused on what really matters, driving lasting change, and engaging people to join in and go with me.

In my own career I have:

- Executed turnarounds that most didn't expect to succeed
- Transformed organizations whose morale started in the dumps
- Built several successful and highly motivated management teams
- Defined and successfully implemented new business strategies

Through these experiences and, more recently, advising many other organizations on implementing their business strategies, I have developed a very practical view of what makes strategies stall and what makes them go. In *MOVE* I will share that formula for how you can get your whole organization to decisively advance your strategy.

A NOTE ABOUT CHANGE VS. TRANSFORMATION

There is much written about leading and managing change and getting through transitions—getting people emotionally bought in, motivated, and ready to change.

In *MOVE* I go beyond the initial change and focus on what it takes to make a transformation really stick after you start the change, for the whole time required to make it happen. But for a moment, let's review what is important about the initial change process.

The Change Equation

Much of the wisdom about motivating an organization to change is referred to in the "formula for change," created by Richard Beckhard and David Gleicher in 1969, and then refined and popularized by Kathie Dannemiller in the early 1990s. It is sometimes called "Gleicher's formula."

If you haven't seen it, this is useful stuff:

$$D \times V \times F > R$$

D = Dissatisfaction with Current State

V = Vision of the Future

F = First Concrete Steps to Get There

R = Resistance to Change

Basically, this equation says that if any one of the things on the left is zero, the resistance, no matter how small, will not be overcome, and the change will not happen.

The most common takeaway from this is that you must make an effort to make sure that D is not zero, meaning if people are too comfortable, they will not change. Dissatisfaction helps motivate change.

But the Harder Part Is in the Middle

What I have found, over and over again, is that even if you get through that initial change and get a good start on it, progress often stalls after a short time, and people go back to what they were doing before.

Even sufficient Dissatisfaction, Vision, and First Concrete Steps are not enough to ensure lasting transformation. Vision defines the exciting goals and end point. First Concrete Steps define the beginning.

And then there is the great, vast abyss in the Middle.

"Are We Still Doing This?"

No matter how vitally important a long-term initiative is to a business, the gravitational pull for people to go back to their day jobs is enormous.

> **The thoughts of not starting, stopping, going back, not changing, and not continuing when it gets tough are so much more powerful and comfortable than the thoughts of *Hey, let's stick with this new, hard thing*.**

To lead a successful transformation, you need to get enough of the people actively moving forward instead of asking, "Are we still doing this?" You also need them to be showing the way forward for others.

I wrote this book to give organizations—the leaders and the whole team—the necessary tools to confront the ongoing hazards of stalled execution at every step along the way.

DOING SOMETHING DIFFERENT

Getting your whole organization to do something different than what they are already doing, and then sticking to it through the "Middle," is one of the most difficult things in business, and it's one of the hardest challenges a leader faces. The Middle is where you need not just desired intentions, but real, defined work to happen.

The Middle is where change can begin to really take hold. When you get very clear about what happens in the Middle, then the whole organization can see the progress, and can believe that you really will achieve the vision at the end. The Middle is where you make it stick. The Middle is the hard part.

The secret (which is not so secret) is that you can *lead* a transformation from the top, but you can't *do* a transformation from the top.

Success lies in getting the whole organization to feel personal ownership in the transformation.

As leaders, we need to figure out how to keep our strategic change alive and moving forward without constant management intervention. How do we make the whole organization not only own the change, but have the ability and the motivation to keep it going?

Inspired by the Gleicher formula, I have created Patty Azzarello's model for successful business transformation: MOVE.

MOVE

The MOVE model is the useful shorthand for the four key elements of a successful business transformation. It defines the four steps for how you get and keep your whole organization moving forward and not asking, "Are we still doing this?"

M Is for the Middle

Strategies are often stated in end goals. An end goal, no matter how inspiring it is, is not enough. The "Middle" is the important part.

A good strategy defines what you will *do*. What you will *do* describes what happens in the Middle and how you will fund, measure, and resource it. In fact, if you want to know what your strategy is, look at your budget. That will speak loud and clear about what you are actually doing regardless of what you say your strategy is.

While you are in the Middle, without the right measures that define your strategy in a concrete way, you can't know if you are making progress. And if you can't see that you are making progress, you will most likely not keep going. Everyone will stay very busy with what they are already doing, and your transformation will stall. The leaders and the team need to get fiercely aligned on the specific, clearly defined, resourced, and sponsored outcomes that need to happen throughout the Middle to bring about the long-term success of your strategy.

O Is for Organization

One of the tough things about a business transformation is that when you initially sign up to do something different, in that moment you still have the same people. Usually the new thing is bigger, more sophisticated, or more challenging in some way. One of the ways I see organizations get stuck is that they try to do the new stuff with the old people. Not everyone will be capable of what the new way requires. Not everyone will be able to step up.

> **Your job as a leader is not to make the best of the team you have, but to build the team you need.**

Everyone in the organization needs to personally invest in understanding what is required and how they can take personal ownership to help lead the change from their roles.

V Is for Valor

This part of the model is about having the grit, persistence, and guts to stick with the change when everyone is losing confidence, questioning you, and presenting emergencies that seem more important in the moment.

> **As a leader, you need to demonstrate your commitment to the transformation with every decision that you make every single day.**

I see too many leaders undermine their strategic initiatives and sacrifice their long-term success by overreacting to short-term pressures. This is another reason why the hard part is in the Middle. Your team will naturally be skeptical, because let's face it, so many strategic initiatives have been abandoned before. Your team will be inclined to wait it out. They may even think that it's a safer bet to wait it out than to start working on new stuff, and risk falling behind when everyone else has switched back to the old stuff. So as a leader, you need to be brave and focused and keep reinforcing decisions to move forward when everyone is tempted to go back or to abandon new work to keep reacting to short-term pressures.

E Is for Everyone

> **Remember, you can lead a transformation from the top, but you can't implement a transformation from the top.**

Success requires everyone—not just management. Everyone. This is critical. To engage everyone requires that you fundamentally change how you think about communicating. Real engagement happens when communication is not just top-down from you, but is a *conversation* that involves *everyone*. You know you have communicated successfully when you are not the only one talking about it! People need to see that their peers have embraced the new strategy before they will feel safe to also get on board. They need to see and feel evidence of transformation throughout the whole Middle, so they will be personally motivated to keep going.

WHY SHOULD YOU READ *MOVE*?

MOVE is a successful leader's execution handbook, but because a key part of the MOVE model is to involve everyone, it is also an important guide for the whole organization. The whole organization will benefit from reading *MOVE* because your transformation must be planned and fueled from the beginning by engaging *everyone* in the process.

CEOs, general managers, leaders of nonprofits, and any manager at any level aspiring to move their business forward will benefit from the ideas, lessons, and real-world examples in *MOVE*. And your whole team will also benefit from understanding what their role is in implementing the business strategy—because you can't get there without them. They actually hold the cards. So invite them in from the beginning.

Where my prior book *RISE* was targeted at individual effectiveness and success, and how to create value and satisfaction in one's career, *MOVE* is targeted at organizational effectiveness and success: how to implement strategy, how to create business value, and how to develop focused, motivated, high-performing teams in one's business.

You and your team could be reading this book because:

- You need to scale your business, but you can't seem to make it happen because everyone is so busy. Your organization has trouble prioritizing.
- You have been talking about important initiatives for a long time, but you are not accomplishing them. You are having trouble getting traction.
- You want to improve how your organization communicates, functions, and executes.
- You want to motivate and engage your team in a more powerful way. You want to see more ownership, accountability, and strategic decision making.
- You have the nagging sense that your business is not reaching its full potential.

THIS BOOK IS NOT ACADEMIC

Everything I talk about in this book is based on real-world experience and examples. If you are looking to learn specific things you can do to MOVE your organization and strategy forward decisively, this is the book for you.

MOVE

PART 1

M = The Middle

Where Transformations Either Happen or Get Stuck

Latin proverb: Virtue is in the middle.

It's easy to get excited at the beginning and define long-term goals at the end. It's the "Middle" that's the problem! It's hard to keep an organization focused on doing something new and difficult for a long time. Since real transformation takes time, you need a strategy to maintain execution and momentum through the Middle.

CHAPTER 1

The Beginning of the Middle

Why New Strategies Stall After the Exciting Kickoff

Before we begin, let's talk about the very first moments of your new strategy. The beginning is great. You are clear, focused, ambitious, ready—and your motivation to move forward seems like the most natural and obvious thing in the world. This new initiative is seriously important to your company and your career. Everyone is on board. You are very committed.

But at this point—at the beginning—it's important to realize that your new strategy is fragile. It hasn't taken hold yet. Think of the launch of your new strategy like your first week of a gym membership: Will you really go to the gym every week and transform your life? Or will you go back to your old habits, and get busy with all the other stuff in your life after the initial inspiration wears off?

What you are facing is the long and vast abyss of the "Middle." The Middle is where the transformation will happen—or not. One of the undeniable realities of the Middle is that it's the long part—and the simple, human fact is that:

> **It's really hard for anyone, not to mention a whole organization, to stay focused and motivated on doing new and difficult things for a long time.**

This is the challenge your business transformation is facing. How will you and your team keep the focus and motivation to do the new, hard work every day, for the next 12–24 months, when it's just so much easier to . . . well . . . not to?

As the leader of a transformation, you are committed and probably feeling substantial pressure to drive this transformation. You may have been brought into this role because others before you have failed. It is very clear in your mind where the business must go, and how it must transform to meet the needs of a changing market or new opportunity. You are ready to forge ahead. So you launch your new strategy with great fanfare in a big, company-wide, all-hands meeting with ice cream . . .

WHAT EVERYONE IS THINKING

I've eaten the ice cream . . .

This is a new thing I'm hearing about for the first time. It sounds like a new important strategy, but who knows for sure. I've seen new strategies come and go; most of the time it doesn't impact my life very much. In a few weeks or months, probably no one will be talking about this anymore. And since I'm already overworked, why bother investing more energy at this point. I'll just wait this one out.

Tell Me If You've Been in This Meeting

You're at a strategic off-site meeting to clarify your new strategy. You talk about the key, long-term things your business must invent, optimize, fix, change, or create. You use the words "game changing" and "innovative" when you talk about these ideas. You may have hired expensive consultants to create your new innovative and game changing strategy. There is tremendous investment, effort, and energy that goes into the beginning of a new strategy. Reaching the point of defining and aligning on a new strategy seems like a huge achievement in itself—and it is.

But then . . .

Everyone goes back to work.
Everyone stays busy on what they were already working on.
The new thing falls victim to the Middle.

The *beginning* is really clear and strong, with lots of investment, excitement, and great intentions. And the *end* is really well defined. But the problem most strategies face is that there is no real plan for the Middle—which is where everything needs to happen!

I have led several successful business transformations in my career. One of the things they all shared was a broken beginning and an inspiring end goal. But as with all transformations they also all shared a long, scary abyss in the Middle.

I learned early on from mentors and trial and error that, if you want to get anything serious done, it's not the goal setting and strategy that is the problem. It's the doing. And the doing is hard because it takes doing for a long time. Without the element of time, there is no real transformation.

It's easy to get an organization focused on a sprint. But in a transformation, you need to keep a whole organization moving in an often unnatural direction for a long period of time. And since human nature is not really built to naturally keep people engaged and focused over a long period of time, to succeed you need to really focus on this ambiguous expanse in the Middle and do many things on purpose to keep people in the game.

Later, in Part 4 (E = Everyone), I'll talk about how I convinced a whole organization of the need for change, and in Part 2 (O = Organization), how I restructured the team; but it's important to note that both of those things, while critical, are still only *beginning* things. Even though creating the right organization and engaging employees required work that is far from obvious and trivial, doing them well still left a long journey through the Middle that no one would be able to see, feel, or measure unless we clearly charted the points along the way to remove the ambiguity.

A GOOD STRATEGY DESCRIBES WHAT YOU WILL *DO* DURING THE MIDDLE

A big reason for the stalls that too often occur in the Middle is that many organizations mistake listing end goals as a strategy: *Our strategy is to double our revenue in these two key market segments. Our strategy is to provide innovative products that create a new market. Our strategy is to develop the strongest indirect channel.*

You become excited about the wonderful achievement at the end, but there is nothing in the definition of that end goal that tells you specifically what to do, which way to go about it, what problems you need to solve, or what you need to fix, change, stop, or invent to get there—these are all things that need to happen in the Middle. These are all things that describe what you will *do*. I'll talk about how to accomplish this in the next chapter: Concrete Outcomes.

LEADERS: EXECUTION IS NOT BENEATH YOU

But first, here is an important point about leading execution. I see so many executives who keep their role in strategy at the big, exciting goal level. Many leaders resist getting involved with execution. It's as though they believe that once they communicate the strategy, people throughout the organization will suddenly understand what new work they have to do; resources will be automatically reassigned without any pain; and individuals will understand how to prioritize new tasks over current work, so it will just get done. It won't.

> **Just because you said what the strategy is, it doesn't mean people will do the right things to implement it.**

Your job at making the strategy come true does not stop after you announce it. One of the hardest things to do is to get an organization to *stop* doing what it is currently doing and *start* doing the different thing that it needs to be doing. You can't just expect your team to find its way through the Middle. Without your involvement, your organization will go back to doing what it is already doing.

As a leader you need to get involved enough in defining outcomes and measures and holding people accountable to specific things, to make sure that the strategy is taking hold and is moving forward through the Middle. Managing execution is not micromanaging, and it is not beneath you.

> **You need to take personal responsibility for what happens in the Middle, because what happens in the Middle is the part where stuff actually gets done!**

I see leaders struggle with two things when it comes to managing execution:

1. **They feel like it's low-level work.** They act as though it's not worth their brilliant strategic time to focus on what people are actually doing. They view execution as a low-level job for other, less important, less strategic people to deal with.
2. **It's hard and boring.** Measuring, tracking, and communicating something that has already been defined is not nearly as exciting as pursuing a big, strategic deal or creating something new.

This "above it all" approach is dangerous. Execution does not happen without leadership involvement. Period.

TEAM: DON'T WAIT—START HELPING

You can choose to wait, or you can choose to proactively help. You can choose to stay in the shadows and be invisible; you can choose to resist or undermine; or you can choose to step forward and help, and to be a bright spot moving the transformation forward.

What strong personal leadership looks like at the beginning of the Middle is keeping yourself educated on the business drivers that are causing the need for this change in the first place. This knowledge will give you the insight and power to lead your own piece of this transformation, and to never be caught off guard by changes you didn't anticipate.

Remember, executive management can lead transformation, but they can't *do* transformation without you. You have a real opportunity to stand out by helping define what is required in your part of the organization through the long Middle. You can stand out by helping your peers get on board as well. The success of the business depends on getting you and enough of your peers and teams to take personal ownership to define and do new things.

> **Don't wait to be asked and certainly don't wait to be pushed. Personal leadership in transformation is important at every level.**

It's not only the job of executive management to think strategically and creatively about implementing strategy. We all must. The following chapters in Part 1 (M = The Middle) will give you the tools to contribute, at a more strategic level, to getting your own team ready to lead your part of the transformation to move the business forward. And by contributing to the forward progress of the business at a more strategic level, you'll add real value and develop your career in the process.

Next

Now that you have started to consider what needs to happen in the Middle, define it in terms of concrete outcomes that will make specific actions obvious.

Read on . . .

CHAPTER 2

Concrete Outcomes

Stop Admiring the Problem and Define Some Specific Actions

You know what you want, and you want your team to do it. You have made the goals clear, and now you are expecting your team to work it out and get it done.

But now somehow there seems to be a stall before you even get started.

You are getting frustrated because your organization does not seem to be moving forward in the new direction even though they all agreed how important it is, and were brought in and even excited about it.

You are beginning to feel that your team is not strategic enough or not taking enough accountability. They are not leading. They are not taking action. They are waiting for more specific operational direction from you, yet you are expecting them to provide that operational direction.

WHAT EVERYONE IS THINKING

This strategy sounds great, but I haven't heard what the new initiatives or priorities are yet. I'm not sure how we are going to achieve this strategy. I haven't been given any different performance objectives. And I haven't been given more resources. It seems that there are a bunch of decisions that executive management still needs to make. And I am fully booked already with current stuff. I'm happy to support the strategy. I'll support it when I know what I'm supposed to do.

> **Simply telling people what is important will not cause the organization to start doing what is important.**

What Happens in the Middle, Exactly?

This is one of the most interesting things that I find in my work with companies on executing their strategies. The problem is not just a communication gap between the executives and the team. . . . **It's that no one anywhere in the organization has articulated what the team needs to do to implement the new strategy.**

Once you launch your new strategy, when everyone wakes up the next morning, what is different—specifically?

> **A company can be really clear about what it wants to accomplish, yet struggle to articulate the specific tasks that will make those goals come true.**

For example, if your goal is to improve market perception, and everyone agrees on that goal, you can't just tell your team, "Go forth and improve market perception." You need to do some work to clarify in what manner you will accomplish that. Will you train your salespeople to engage differently? Will you change your marketing message? Will you improve your relationships with market analysts and media? Will you change your product? Will you create a new customer service offer?

When I take management teams through my Strategy into Action program, this lack of clarity about what the organization needs to do in the "Middle" is what we focus on the most. We shine a big spotlight on defining what the specific approach is in the Middle to make the end goals come true. I have taken countless leadership teams through this process, and this basic idea about strategy always works:

> **A strategy must describe what you will *do*, including how you will measure and resource it. Strategy must clarify specific action.**

An end goal, no matter how inspiring it is, is not enough to mobilize an organization. What it gives you is a list of wishes, not an actual strategy. But by insisting that your strategy describes what you will *do*, you will by definition be making it clear what things need to happen in the Middle.

MOVING FROM BIG, VAGUE END GOALS TO ACTIONABLE STRATEGY

Think about the really important goals your team talks about all the time. When you talk about them everyone agrees they are critical: *We must improve quality. We must innovate. We must respond to a competitive threat. We must evolve our business model to provide better service.*

Talk vs. Action

To move your team from talking about important stuff in a vague way to actually making progress on these things in a real way, the first step is to realize that you are stuck because you are still only *talking*.

You need to change the nature of the conversation to become one that drives action, instead of just more talking. One of the biggest hazards to watch for is a concept called "smart talk."

The term was coined by Bob Sutton and Jeffrey Pfeffer in their *Harvard Business Review* article, "The Smart Talk Trap" (May–June 1999), and it so richly describes what happens when smart people substitute talking for action:

> We found that a particular kind of talk is an especially insidious inhibitor of organizational action: "smart talk." The elements of smart talk include sounding confident, articulate, and eloquent; having interesting information and ideas; and possessing a good vocabulary. But smart talk tends to have other, less benign components: first, it focuses on the negative, and second, it is unnecessarily complicated or abstract (or both). In other words, people engage in smart talk to spout criticisms and complexities. Unfortunately, such talk has an uncanny way of stopping action in its tracks. That's why we call this dynamic the *smart-talk trap*.

This is a specific and unfortunately common type of corporate behavior where people substitute *sounding smart in a meeting* for *actually contributing work.* I'm certain you know some of these people!

These people will come to meetings with lots of insight and data. They will always be ready to shed more light on the problem by providing details, benchmarks, and customer examples. They will have lots of smart stuff to say. Everyone will think, "Wow, they're really smart."

Describing the "Situation"

It's vitally important as a leader to recognize when your team is falling into the pattern of accepting smart sounding ideas and inputs instead of measurable forward progress. The most effective way I have found to break through this is to recognize when you get stuck in a pattern of smart-talking about the "situation."

Groups of people have a very strong tendency to discuss the situation—a lot. Over and over again. For a really long time. Situation conversations are the easiest conversations to have because there is no risk. You are simply stating facts. You might contribute facts that no one else knows, and you might sound really smart while saying them, but the fact of the matter is that there is no forward progress because you are simply describing what is happening.

Situation discussions describe *what we are doing, what the market is doing, what the competitors are doing, what the investors are saying, what the problems are, what the costs are, what the customers are demanding, what the changes in business model are causing, what the opportunities are, what the employees are doing and not doing.* Situation discussions don't go anywhere; they only gather more detail. With a ready supply of smart talk, the situation discussion will be colorfully augmented by someone saying, "Well, this is an even more critical problem than we thought because I just got back from Asia and saw this . . ."; or, "This is even harder because I learned our competitors are launching their new version this quarter. . . ." More and more smart talk gets added, and the situation discussion turns into a bigger and bigger situation hairball.

Sure, it's important to use some time to note and understand the situation, but you can just feel it when everyone has internalized the situation and then . . . you keep talking about it! Talking and talking and talking about it. You can feel it in your stomach when the meeting is not going anywhere, and you're still talking. The talk gets smarter and smarter and the forward motion everyone is craving never happens.

Situation discussions are basically this: collectively admiring the problem.

Situation vs. Outcome

The way to break through this type of stall is to train your team members to catch themselves having a situation discussion, and then say, "Let's stop talking about the *situation* and let's try to define an *outcome* that we want to achieve."

For example, one of the most common situation discussions that I guarantee is happening hundreds of times at this very moment in business meetings around the world is the following "mother of all situation" discussions:

> This is very important, but we don't have enough resources to do it.

Here is a specific version. We need to improve the quality of our product to be more competitive, but all of our resources are tied up on creating new features. We can't fall behind on features, and we have no extra resources. But we really need to improve quality. But we don't have the budget . . . and around and around.

Instead of adding fur to that situation discussion, let's take this situation discussion and turn it into an outcome discussion. Here is an example. Note how resisting situation talk allows the discussion to move forward:

- Okay. We can't afford to fix all the quality problems, so let's stop talking about this in a vague way. Let's talk about some concrete things we can do on a smaller scale that would make a positive difference. Which quality problems are having the most negative business impact right now?

- There are two issues in the user interface that our biggest customers are complaining about. (Situation)
- How about if we fix those two problems first? (Outcome proposal)
- But that doesn't take into account the issue in Europe. The quality issues in Europe are related to difference in governance laws. (Situation)
- I suggest we fix only the top one issue in the United States right away, but we fix the top three in Europe now too (Outcome proposal), as we have more pipeline held up in Europe.
- But that doesn't solve our overall quality problems, which are related to the fundamental structure of our product, which I have assessed is slowing our sales pipeline growth by 20 percent. (Smart talk. Rat hole. Situation)
- What outcome do you suggest we target to solve that particular point? (Challenge to smart talk)
- I don't know, we just need to fix it. It's really important. (Situation. Stall)
- That is still situation discussion. How about we fix the problems we just listed first, and right away we train the sales force on how to help customers work around these platform issues temporarily? (Outcome proposal)
- But when can we fix the main platform? We don't have the resources to do it. (Age-old situation)
- Let's look at doing a platform release one year from now. After we fix this initial round of quality issues and release this current round of features, we then prioritize the platform changes and get it done. (Outcome proposal)
- But if we do that, we'll fall behind our competitors in functionality again. (Shut up. Situation)
- We need to agree that if the platform change is a priority, we must get it accomplished no matter what our level of resources—even if we need to move resources from the work to add new functionality. (Outcome proposal)
- We will work with marketing and sales to improve our conversion rate in the part of our pipeline that is with customers not currently affected by the platform issue. (Outcome proposal)

Note the difference between situation and outcome conversation.

Outcome discussions can be long and painful too, but the big difference is that they are going somewhere. Outcome conversation is productive conversation. It leads to action.

Outcome vs. Next

There are many other benefits to moving from situation conversations to outcome conversations. One of the other great things about outcome-oriented conversations is that they can be used to resolve disputes. When you are talking about a situation and what to do next, "next" is a concept fraught with opinion and emotion. It might involve someone giving something up or stopping something. It might involve doing or learning something new. "Next" has all the personal investment of the present wrapped up in it. So to get people to agree about what to do next if a clear outcome is not defined, there could be a million possible choices, all laden with personal investment, experience, insight, opinion, and emotion.

But instead you can pick a point in the future and say, "Let's describe that point. Let's agree on that point in the future." Suddenly everyone's focus is shifted away from their invested and urgent personal space, and it is placed on a goal that is in the distance. It breaks the emotional stranglehold of something that threatens to change right now.

The other benefit is that if you can agree on what the point in the future looks like, it reduces the set of possible next steps from a million to several. There are far fewer choices of what to do next to serve a well-defined outcome. You can have a much more focused and productive debate.

Describe What It Looks Like When It Is Working

To force the conversation to be about concrete outcomes can be a difficult skill to master. But it is worth the effort. It's the only way to move decisively forward.

If your group is having trouble with this, here is something you can try. When I'm working with a team that can't seem to get their minds around which outcome to focus on, I ask them to simply describe what it looks like when it is working. If the desired outcome were working the way you needed it to be, what would you see? What would be happening? What would people be saying and doing? What would employees, customers, partners, analysts, and media be saying? What would they be experiencing?

Once you start describing what the concrete desired outcome looks like when it is working, you will be able to land the plane. For example, I was working with a team who needed to execute a successful product migration from an old version to a new version. They naturally started talking about the situation, the complexity, the expense, the possibility of customer attrition. . . . But when I encouraged them to start describing desired outcomes, one person said, "We'd have enough customers successfully using the new version by February 1." Then others added these descriptions: "There would be a combination of existing and new customers successfully using the new version"; "Existing small and mid-size customers would be motivated and volunteer to migrate on their own"; "Our largest customers would be confident to migrate because they felt guided and supported by us to make sure their migration was successful."

By focusing on describing what it would look like if it were working, they were able to define outcomes that were concrete enough to suggest the specific necessary actions. This is another wonderful thing about outcome conversation. When you get concrete in your language about outcomes, the action plan just falls out in a very clear way. In this example, the team quickly got to a list of actions to create a self-migration program for small and mid-size customers, a personally delivered program for large customers, and a marketing campaign for new customers.

Trap: Avoiding Action—"But It Doesn't Solve the Whole Problem"

One of the other mistakes I see teams making is that when they work on big problems, even if they focus on describing outcomes, the outcomes are too big—and then they decide it's impossible.

Here is an example of such a desired outcome: We need to do a better job running meetings in our organization. What would it look like if it were working? All meetings would start and finish on time and have a clear purpose and desired outcomes defined, the right people would be in attendance, and we'd document decisions and actions.

Then they start to think about all the reasons why this won't work in certain organizations or geographies, or that there is not enough sponsorship, or that there are too many different kinds of meetings to make a new process work.

Then one brave soul will stand up and say something like, "Why don't we start by improving our quarterly business review meetings? Let's describe what those would look like if they were working better."

Then someone else will shoot that down and say, "But that doesn't solve the whole problem," or "that doesn't solve the biggest part of the problem."

Resist this type of reasoning.

Solve the smaller, concrete problem. Then pick another small concrete problem and solve that one next.

Don't let the reasoning of "but this doesn't solve the whole problem" stop you from making progress on a valuable, smaller, concrete problem.

This destructive immune response happens for a few reasons. People can convince themselves that if the big problem is impossible, then it's okay not to try. *Why waste time on something that is impossible?* But the real issue is fear of actually doing something. Once you commit to defining a specific, concrete problem that can be solved, then it becomes clear what you need to do—and you need to do it.

There is a lot of avoidance of *doing* that happens in business, because it's easier to pretend to add value by just talking about the complexity of the big problem and sounding smart, and stating all the reasons why it can't be done.

Concrete, specific outcomes drive action. Always beware of people who are experts at avoiding action.

Drive Forward Momentum by Getting Concrete and Specific

What is the difference between an outcome that helps drive action, and an end goal (also an outcome) that does not drive action? The answer is *scope* and *concreteness*. Where a big, inspiring end goal is too high-level and vague to drive action, a more tightly defined, concrete, specific outcome will make your action plan very clear.

I'll share a real example of how powerful this approach of defining concrete, specific outcomes can be for your business.

I was doing a Strategy into Action session for a company that made consumer electronics products. They were having a revenue issue in Europe—an issue they had had (and talked about) for more than a year. This was put on a list of strategic initiatives. In their old habits, they would discuss the fact that "there is a problem in Europe." There would be lots of talk about why, and how difficult it was, and that they didn't have enough sales resources. (Situation)

Then at some point, the meeting would end. The European manager would be on the hook for the improvement, and then would come back the next quarter and report once again that the numbers for Europe were less than they needed. There was a sense of resignation among the team that Europe was a problem in general, and that it was not solely the fault of the Sales GM who was highly competent. There were circumstances that made this challenging, and so on and so on . . . (Situation!)

Since I had only one day to help them, I was more impatient. I got them talking about possible concrete outcomes instead of the situation.

This discussion lasted for a couple of hours and there was more to it, but I've simplified it and noted some highlights that demonstrate the importance of taking the approach of forcing the conversation to be about concrete outcomes. My part is in *italics*.

- *Okay. So more revenue in Europe . . . how much more are we talking about?*
- CEO: $20 million a year.
- *If you were getting that revenue, where do you believe it would be coming from? Can it come from your current customers and market?*

- Sales GM: No, probably not.
- *Then where? If the revenue problem were solved, what would be happening?*
- Sales GM: It would be coming through the retail channel. The market has shifted. Enterprise is not as significant anymore.
- *Okay. So are we saying that a desired outcome is that the incremental revenue in Europe of $20 million a year will come from the retail channel?*
- Sales GM: No, probably 75 percent.
- *Okay. So $15 million needs to come from the retail channel and $5 million from the current enterprise markets. What will be happening that increases the current model in enterprise by $5 million?*
- Sales GM: I'm comfortable that my current plan addresses that.
- *Okay. Then what would be true if there was $15 million coming from retail? Do you have any revenue coming from retail channels?*
- Sales GM: No. Not at this time.
- *So one outcome you need is to have a functioning retail channel. Do you need to have a retail channel in every country you currently serve or could you get the $15 million from fewer countries?*
- Sales GM: I believe we could get that revenue if we had retail success in the UK, France, and Germany.
- *What does retail success look like in the UK, France, and Germany? If that were working, what would be happening?*
- We would be a preferred vendor in the retail outlets of the top four providers in those countries. The retail salespeople would be recommending and selling our products.
- *What would be true if that was happening? What would you need to fix, build, or invent to get retail salespeople recommending and selling your products?*
- CMO: We would need to have marketing programs that work for those retail outlets, and we would need someone managing those partnerships.
- *Can your sales force do that?*

- Sales GM: No. I only have an enterprise sales force. They have no retail experience, and they are not marketing people.
- *So if you want that outcome, what needs to happen?*
- Note: CMO and Business Development now get involved:
- CMO: We need to create a retail marketing and sales channel in Europe.
- *Do you have anyone in your organization that can create retail partnerships and marketing programs in the UK, France, and Germany?*
- Sales GM: No. This is a very particular skill set. I don't have those skills on my team.
- CMO: We could use some of the content from our U.S. programs, but it would need to be highly localized, and tuned for each partner. Do you think that one Europe-based partner expert could handle all three countries?
- Sales GM: No. The situations and cultures are so different in each country, I believe that we would need a local partner specialist in each country.
- *Is the opportunity the same in all three countries?*
- Business Development: I expect more than half of the revenue would come from Germany. I think we should start with Germany.
- Sales GM: I agree, Germany will be at least 50 percent of the revenue.
- CMO: When we were hiring a marketing person in Europe last quarter, I interviewed someone whose expertise was retail marketing. She was not a fit at the time, but she would be good to talk to now.
- Sales GM: Do I have permission to restructure the sales force?
- CEO: Yes, show me the plan to get the retail marketing established to drive this $15 million of revenue.

Once you get a group of people talking about concrete desired outcomes instead of situations or vague high-level goals, a few wonderful and remarkable things happen.

1. **More information comes out.**

Without having this concrete-outcome oriented conversation, there would not have been a discussion about the retail channel or having the wrong sales force. The sales GM was trying to make do with the resources he had, and since he was not personally an expert in retail, he was not inclined to go there.

Simply by asking questions—*What would be happening if your goal was met? What would it look like?*—and shifting our discussion to force ourselves to discuss concrete outcomes, it made the need for a strategy change really clear. The revenue was not going to come from the existing enterprise sales force. Let's once and for all stop hoping for that. The needed retail strategy might seem obvious to you at this point, but it was simply not being discussed by this management team until we stopped talking about the situation (revenue is too low in Europe, and it's a really hard problem) and started talking about a concrete outcome (successful retail channels exist in France, the UK, and Germany).

2. **The action plan builds itself.**

Once you start defining concrete outcomes, you move to a very obvious and specific list of things that must be done. Before the outcome conversation, they would have once again let the Sales GM go back to Europe and would have hoped for an increase in revenue. He might have tried new enterprise marketing programs or fine-tuned sales comp plans or incentives. Simply by asking a question—*What do you need to fix, build, or invent to get this outcome?*—they easily created the list. When you define the outcome in a concrete enough way, the necessary actions just fall out. In this example the obvious actions were:

- Hire a retail marketing person in Germany
- Recruit the top four retail partners in Germany
- Launch a partner marketing and business plan in Germany
- Initiate campaigns in Germany
- Recruit partner marketing experts in the UK and France
- Identify the top enterprise salespeople and adjust quotas
- Complete the sales force restructuring

3. **People can figure out how to contribute.**

Another really interesting thing I see happen, when teams stop discussing situations and vague end goals and start defining concrete outcomes, is that people who have otherwise been silent now can see how they can contribute. When this was simply the problem of the sales GM, the discussion was between only the sales GM and the CEO. When the discussion moved to the concrete outcome of establishing a successful retail channel in three countries in Europe, others on the team could see exactly how and what they could contribute to that.

Getting your team to define concrete outcomes unlocks a lot more of the power of your team.

Caution: Concrete Conversation About Outcomes Will Cause Conflict

Moving from big goals to concrete descriptions of outcomes is really hard work. Good outcome conversation has concrete elements and proposals in it. It's scary because as soon as you become concrete, you are committing to doing something specific—and as soon as you choose to do something specific, you could be wrong. And it's also scary because being concrete and specific invites conflict. If you say, "We are going to roll out this program this year," everyone can agree. But if you get specific and concrete and say, "We are going to roll out this program first only in North America this year, and move 10 people from product development to support the implementation, and therefore delay the release of the next product for three months . . . ," that gives people something to disagree about!

As a leader, it's important to realize that this type of productive conflict is a good and necessary thing.

Avoiding being concrete to avoid conflict means that you are also avoiding action.

If you start by trying to avoid conflict, you will lock yourself in an ever-growing conversation about situations and lofty end goals, and your forward progress on important things will stall. Get really clear.

Don't trade conflict-free comfort in the moment for actually moving forward. I talk about how to deal with these types of conflicts in Chapter 20: Clarity and Conflict.

NEXT

Pay careful attention to the overall timeline. The temptation to think there is a lot of time to work on a long-term initiative is a false comfort that results in failed execution. Plot each step through the Middle, and get everyone ready to *move* now.

Read on . . .

CHAPTER 3

Timing and Momentum

Maintaining a Sense of Urgency for a Long Time

THE FORECAST IS HAZY . . .

Now you are somewhere in the "Middle." There is work getting done. But something is missing. The motivation for the new work is hard to see. The excitement from the beginning is waning as all of the present activity re-asserts itself. You are frustrated that the strategy is not moving forward in a decisive way. There are some stalls—some late or lethargic starts. You can't feel forward momentum and urgency and you are starting to worry . . .

WHAT EVERYONE IS THINKING

"Did we start yet?" It seems like I heard some stuff about that a while ago. . . . I haven't really noticed a change so far. My job is the same. We still have all the same problems. Oh well, as I understand it, this was a long-term strategy, so maybe we didn't really kick it off yet. In any case, I don't need to worry about it for a while because we have a lot of time."

FOCUS ON MID-TERM CHECKPOINTS

There is a strong organizational tendency for people to think that they don't have to worry about anything in month 1 of an 18-month initiative.

When people focus only on the long-term end goal, then the first step in their long-term journey is a delay. It's important to create a framing of the initiative in a way that avoids this early sense of complacency.

In the last chapter we talked about the importance of defining concrete outcomes. The next tool to keep everyone on track through the Middle is *timing*. Once you have defined concrete outcomes that will enable your long-term goal, you need to get your team to define smaller, mid-term checkpoints and deliverables that are necessary at *specific mid-points all the way through* the Middle, *to achieve your desired outcomes.*

By placing these clear, mid-term checkpoints on a timeline, you will create the light posts that the organization needs in order to see where they are going through the long Middle—and to keep going. These become not only your mid-term checkpoints, but also your enablers of urgency—if you place them on a timeline so they occur at an aggressive pace, you will be creating the urgency you desire. Whenever I see an executive say, "I want to see a sense of urgency," I always wonder what, specifically, they want to see. Do they want to see people running around in a panic? Would that make them feel better? **If you want urgency, define urgency by what you put on the timeline.**

One of the biggest challenges of the Middle, because it's so long, is to simply know where you are at any point in time. Without these mid-term check points, while you are in the Middle you won't be able to know if you are making progress. Ten months into an 18-month initiative, the progress might not yet be palpable. And if everyone can't see and feel that you are making progress, they will most likely not keep going. You will lose momentum. People will ask, "Are we still doing this?" Your strategic progress will stall.

Stage the Mid-term Checkpoints Out Over a Timeline

There is a pretty simple approach to accomplish this, and it is profoundly helpful. This is the same process I use when I take teams through my Strategy into Action process.

For each of the concrete outcomes you have defined, create a blank timeline and work through the following questions with your team.

Let's imagine that your timeline is one year. (You can do this for a timeline of any duration.):

1. What will we measure at the end (12 months out)? This is the easy part. Everyone loves an end goal!

2. If we have achieved that outcome, what must be true/done/ existing nine months out? What will we *see*? (Put the third-quarter mid-point outcome on the timeline.)

3. If that is true at nine months, what must we have finished at the halfway point? What will we *see*? What will we measure at the halfway point to ensure we are on track? (Put the mid-point outcome on the timeline.)

4. If that is true at the six-month mark, what needs to be defined, planned, and started at the three-month mark? What will we *see*? (Put the three-month outcome on the timeline.)

5. If that needs to be done in three months, then what do we need to start now?

"WHAT WILL WE *SEE*?"

"What will we *see*?" is a very powerful and focusing question. By forcing the team to define mid-point milestones that you can see, you are, in fact, building a good strategy that describes what you will *do* throughout the Middle. Things you can see are concrete. Describing the right mid-term checkpoints will point to specific, prioritized work.

Example: "Sell Higher"

For example, your goal is to "sell higher" in your enterprise accounts. That is your big, vague end goal. You have, then, also defined your strategy in terms of concrete outcomes to be: 50 new executive level relationships and 5 big deals closed by the end of the first year. Even though that is more concrete than "we need to sell higher," that only measures what it looks like when it is done, not what it needs to look like along the way.

So what happens is that everyone nods their heads and goes back to work. Nothing changes. You've got plenty of time. Kevin is working on a plan. Business still comes in. Everyone is busy and that's the end of that. By the time Kevin is ready to present the plan, there is no longer an appetite for it because everyone is busy.

But if you force yourself to define (at the beginning) what you will see at the mid-points before you send Kevin off to create a plan, you can keep everyone focused. For example: At three quarters out, what you could *see* is that there are 30 new big deals under discussion, and 10 of them are officially in the pipeline. Then you ask, for that to be true nine months out, what would need to be true in six months? In six months we could *see* that 50 target accounts are defined and 50 executives are named, and each one has a salesperson assigned and a quota for the next 18 months.

Then you need to ask, for that to be true six months out, what will need to be true one quarter out? What would we *see*? Well, that might be that 100 accounts are selected for vetting, and that 25 sales reps in North America where you decide to pilot the program have gone through a training, and have found an external mentor who can help them up their sales skill level.

If that were true one quarter out, that means that one month out, you need to have identified these first 25 sales reps and created a headhunting firm of sorts to help match them up with external mentors.

Do you notice the difference? Without this process, people leave the meeting nodding their heads and thinking, *Yeah, that's important, but we have a year to get it done, so I don't need to worry about it for a while.* When you get a task that will take a year, on any Monday early in the process, you kind of still have a year. If you don't start it for a month, you still have most of the year. But this thinking can repeat over and over again. Suddenly you are 10 months in and still have 12 months of work left to do.

But if instead you define the timeline up front, and you leave the meeting with checkpoints already defined for three, six, and nine months out, people leave the meeting with specific actions that need to be done as soon as one month out!

People can't simply just go back to work and feel like they have a year to make it come true. They have tasks to do starting immediately!

Long-term initiatives suffer from what feels like an abundance of time in the beginning. So it requires that the leader in charge stays diligent about guiding people through the Middle with the right, concrete, mid-term checkpoints.

SHINE A SPOTLIGHT ON THE MIDDLE, CONSISTENTLY . . . FOR A LONG TIME

The Middle is also dangerous simply because it is long. We can all more easily deal with important things that take a short time. We get the feeling, "I can do that," because when we can see the beginning, the Middle, and the end of something all at once we know how to finish it. **Keeping progress going on an initiative or transformation that spans months or years is really hard for any human or team because you can't see the whole thing right now.**

When I use this approach with leadership teams of working backwards from the due date and defining concrete outcomes—defining and committing to things you can *see* along the way, we often go from the team thinking they have plenty of time to realizing that they are already late! When you create a timeline of specific concrete, *see*-able checkpoints through the Middle, strategic progress and a sense of urgency are ensured because you have clearly mapped it out.

CREATE A TIMELINE

One communication tool that I have found to be enormously helpful to illuminate the path through the Middle is a simple timeline that articulates the strategy and the key milestones (the things you can *see*) along the way throughout the Middle. I always have a timeline with me that looks something like Figure 3.1.

Building Your Communications Timeline

1. Always have a "You Are Here" mark on your timeline.
2. Make sure that mark is never all the way to the left. It's kind of soul destroying to see that everything that needs to be done is still ahead of you. Having the "You Are Here" mark

Figure 3.1   Timeline Communication Tool

somewhere toward the Middle is less discouraging. And it lets
you create context. It let's you acknowledge people for the
work that was done already, and it shows what the future work
is building on.

3. Put big general milestones and defined control points that
   everyone can relate to below the line.
4. Put specific initiatives or critical tasks to be accomplished
   above the line.

Once you have created this communication tool, use it
over and over again. Pull it out every time you communicate
about what you are doing. Update it and show the "You are
here" dot moving to the right, and list the finished accomplishments to the left of it. Keep the same future initiatives on the
page. After people see this 20 or 100 times they will start to
think two things: First, I guess we are making progress even
though I can't see it from my desk; and second, I guess we are
serious about that stuff on the right because it's not going away.

Using a timeline like this as a communication tool is one of the best
defenses against the dreaded question: "Are we still doing this?"

As we'll talk about in Part 3 (V = Valor) and Part 4 (E = Everyone),
your team will need you to let them know you are serious—over and
over (and over and over) again. **Each time you show the timeline, one
less person will be asking, "Are we still doing this?" and will just
start doing it.**

Next

Now that you have points on the timeline to measure, note that the wrong measures can take your strategy in the wrong direction. Choose measures that will ensure material progress on the right things. Read on . . .

CHAPTER 4

Control Points

Metrics That Drive Action on the Right Things

How Do We Measure Success?

Leaders at every level often ask me, "What should I be measuring?" This is an area where frankly many leaders feel inadequate. You are measuring stuff, but have the sense that the metrics are not giving you the full picture, or the most important part of the picture. It makes you nervous. You think, *I need to know how we are doing. I need to reduce risk. To be an effective leader, I need to make sure that we are measuring and tracking progress, but I don't feel satisfied with the information I have.*

It's hard to figure out what to measure, so you can feel confident you are tracking progress and risks, but not spending so much time tracking and measuring everything that you are micromanaging.

What Everyone Is Thinking

I'm not sure I fully understand the strategy, but I do understand my measures, so I will tune my work to optimize what I'm being measured on. I'll keep delivering and reporting on these measures unless someone tells me otherwise.

Good Measures and Bad Measures

The right measures are so important. If you can get it right, you can achieve the holy grail of being confident about progress without getting overly involved in tracking detail. But just like there are end goals masquerading as good strategy, there are often bad measures standing in for truly meaningful ones. At a top level here is how I classify good and bad measures:

- Bad measures: Activities and details
- Good measures: Control points and outcomes

Many times we select bad measures simply because they are the easiest thing to measure. We placate ourselves with the fact that we are measuring something. But, in fact, we may be doing more harm than good.

Good measures predict actual desired outcomes and enable you to move the business forward. Bad measures measure only activities or steps in the process, not outcomes. Here's a basic example of what I mean. Imagine your goal is to improve the performance of customer service reps, so you put them all through customer service training. If you have a success measure of "# of customer service reps who have gone through training," that is a measure of the *activity*—that they have gone through the training. It tells you literally nothing about whether or not they have become better at their jobs.

And sometimes the bad measures not only fail to show the true picture, they can actually incent the wrong behaviors and outcomes. Bad measures can cause stalls, delays, and wrong work—even though on some level they make you feel good because you are measuring something.

Let me describe some common bad measures. Customer service and support is a good example to discuss good and bad measures, because it is an area in most businesses that has explicit measures.

First, here are some examples of common customer service and support measures:

- How many customer service calls did you close out?
- How many problems did you fix?
- How fast did you fix the problem?

These kind of measures are tempting because obviously, you'd like to serve a lot of customers, fix as many problems as possible, and do it quickly. Many organizations show good results on these measures.

But these are bad measures because you can have good performance against these measures and still have unhappy customers who are not referring your products or willing to buy more. These are bad measures because they only relate to process steps and activities:

- *Number of closed customer calls* is a process step (an activity). It does not convey a measure of happy customers (and actual outcome), only that the call was closed.

- *Number of problems fixed* is activity again. It does not offer any qualitative view or insight as to whether those were resolutions for key problems that important customers cared about. *The most important issues from the most important customers* are the important things you want to measure. Fixing any one issue for any customer is just an activity.

- *Speed to fix it* is another measure of a process stop, not an outcome measure. It does not offer any insight into how effective the fix was, or if the fix made the customer happy.

In addition, the existence of bad measures can make an organization ignore what they should be measuring because they feel satisfied that they are measuring something. But the outcome of measuring process steps and activities is not the right outcome for these reasons:

1. They fail to measure the most necessary and relevant outcome: How are we doing on the things that are most important to our customers who are referring us or buying more?
2. They de-motivate good behavior that might actually help customer satisfaction.

Here are some examples of how bad measures can create bad behaviors and outcomes.

Bad Customer Service Measure #1: Measuring Speed

While the idea of fixing problems fast seems like a good idea, it's important to understand that the measure of speed can cause your support team to actually ignore underlying customer problems, because the measure motivates service reps to close out problems in the system quickly instead of taking the time to actually fix them.

This is what you get: I maximized my measure. I got the customer off the phone quickly (and annoyed the customer). Spending the necessary time to work with the customer (actual service) would result in a poor service score because the service rep spent too much time.

Bad Customer Service Measure #2: Measuring Quantity

Again, while the idea of fixing as many customer issues as possible seems like a good idea, I've seen it backfire where a simple problem exists that comes up a lot. Since your measure is the number of customer issues resolved, if it is fast and easy for the service rep to resolve the problem every time it happens, the service staff will benefit from leaving it broken, because fixing it over and over again quickly is a good way to up their numbers.

Here is what you get: a high issue-resolved count and lots of annoyed customers because you never fix lingering issues in your product or service.

Defining Good Measures/Behaviors

So, to continue with our customer service example, what would be an alternative good measure for customer service?

To figure that out, first think about the actual outcome you desire—even if it seems hard to measure. How about this: *We want our top customers to be satisfied enough with our product and service to refer or re-purchase.*

**If that is the case, then why not make the measure:
How many of our top customers are satisfied
enough to refer or re-purchase?**

But this seems hard to measure. Let's think about it. How could you get this measure? What exactly could you measure?

Resist the tendency to give up here! Don't give up because it seems hard to measure and go back to a bad, easy-to-measure measure. To come up with a truly effective measure requires a combination of rigor and creativity. Talk about it with your team and challenge them to come up with measures that actually measure the outcome you want.

How about if each executive calls two customers/month and asks, "Are you satisfied with how the product works and the service you receive? What would it take to make you satisfied enough to refer us or to re-purchase?" You could require your customer service reps to ask the same thing on each phone call or chat. Collect that data.

This issue of the wrong measures came loud and clear for me when I was general manager of a large business unit. There was a stretch of time where it seemed every week a sales rep invited me to have lunch at the fancy corporate HQ customer briefing center with a visiting customer. I'd ask the sales rep, "Are there any issues I should know about?" They would answer, "No, it's just a lunch." Before I went, I'd run the official customer satisfaction data on the customer— every time the survey results showed "all good."

Then I'd sit down to lunch and before I could take a bite, I'd get my head ripped off. These customers were not merely dissatisfied; they were livid! They were at the end of their rope, downright hostile, and very, very angry—usually for a good reason—because their key issues had been ignored for a really long time (even though all of our measures about their satisfaction gave us a good score).

It turns out they had been calling customer support for months and telling them, "The system is not doing what we bought it for." The calls were being handled in a manner that the service rep would say, "I'm sorry," and after asking some rudimentary questions about basic operation (presumably, "Is the device plugged in, and is it retaining its original mass and color?"), and after the service rep decided that it was working as expected, they would close the call out. After months of this, the customers were really angry that no one was listening to them, while at the same time our support staff were all overachieving on their metrics.

LIMPING COWS AND CONTROL POINTS

You can review activities for eons and never really get a true feel for whether or not your business is moving forward. *You just make your organization really competent at collecting and reviewing data.* The answer is for the organization to work together to define key *control points*.

To explain the concept of measuring control points vs. activities or process steps I want to first reference Temple Grandin, a scientist and leading consultant in agriculture. One of the things she has done in her work is to create an animal welfare audit for the U.S. Department of Agriculture. In her book *Animals in Translation* (Scribner, 2005), she talks about this idea of measuring process steps (activities) vs. control points (outcomes) in a very compelling way:

> For instance, one thing I want to know is whether the animals' legs are sound. There are lots of things that can affect a cow's ability to walk: bad genes, poor flooring, too much grain in the feed, foot rot, poor hoof care, rough treatment of the animals . . .

Her measures focus only on outcomes and control points—and they specifically don't focus on details and process steps.

She talks about how most regulators will try and measure (and regulate) all of these things, where all she cares about is a simple 10-point audit of plainly observable things like "Are the cows limping?" She compares this simple outcome-oriented audit to the typical government audits that measure hundreds of things.

There are three common problems with measuring activities, process steps, and details that the "limping cows" approach solves. You can see why this is so brilliant and such a marvelous example of picking the right type of measure that creates a control point. **If the cows are limping (one outcome), the plant fails the whole audit:**

1. **Measuring Process Steps, Not Outcomes**

   The only way a plant can then pass the audit is to figure out why the cows are limping and get it fixed. This could be one, a few, or many things. The specific reason (activities and details) doesn't really matter, such as if the floor is slippery, or the feed is wrong, or the hoof care is intermittent. Whatever the problem is, if the cows are no longer limping, she knows the right things got fixed and she never needed to know the details. The right outcome is achieved.

I love this example of a control point: She defined the one outcome that must be true. Then the group needs to manage all the details, activities, and process steps to make it come true. As long as the outcome is true, she never needs to know all the details—with another important implication being: We don't have to drag details up and down the organization to get a good insight. (See Chapter 19: Detail: The Momentum Killer.)

2. **Hiding in Complexity**

As Temple Grandin also clearly states: "When a plant fails 1 critical item out of 10, it's easy to fail the whole plant. But when it fails that same item on a list of 100, it doesn't look so bad. I find the same thing happens in business." **Organizations get so busy measuring too many things at a detailed level that they have no insight at all about what the important things driving the business even are.**

When you get mired in detailed measures of activities and process steps, it's tough to say how bad is bad, or how good is good. Measuring too many details obscures knowing the thing you truly need to know: What is the fundamental outcome you need, and are you getting it?

3. **Measuring the Paper, Not the Reality**

Another important aspect of Temple Grandin's point of view on control points is that having too many reviews and checklists creates a tendency to audit to records "on paper," and you can lose track of what is actually happening in the real world.

In my earlier example, all the paper reporting on customer satisfaction was great. But the customer was angry. We were measuring the details about the product basics and the process steps of taking and closing out calls. It all looked good on paper—we passed the audit, but were not even looking for the limping cows. The customers were hurting. It could have been for one or many reasons, but we didn't know because we didn't look. We didn't ask. We didn't listen. We were too satisfied with our measures of process activities and details on paper.

What Are Your "Limping Cows"?

Think about your business. For each project, what are the right control points to measure? **What are those few things that if they turn out right—everything turns out right?**

It's important to pick something that is at a higher level than a detail or process step (how many calls did we make?), but is also not a big, vaguely defined end goal (more revenue).

What are one or two key outcome/control-point–oriented measures that will tell you whether or not your project is really on track? Let me give you some examples.

Customer Experience Example: Control Point = "Fun in 15 Minutes"

One of my favorite examples of motivating the right behavior by picking the right control point was a story about how I got a team of engineers to make progress on something important that they didn't care about.

I was managing a software development team of about 200 people. Our product had an absolutely dreadful user interface, and the worst part was the initial experience. Installing it could make you want to kill yourself. It was very cumbersome to do, and if you got one step wrong in a sequence of 23 steps, or did something out of order, there was no recovery. You had to start over.

I wanted to get this fixed. But to an engineer, asking them to work on installation problems is like asking them to cut their leg off. Not only did they not care about this problem, they were actively avoiding even looking at it because it was such a boring problem to work on. At the time, we were not measuring control points, which in this case would be something related to "How long does it take a customer to achieve success?"

Instead we were only measuring process steps and details. The engineers' quality improvements were only being measured by "severity of problem." Level 1 and 2 problems were things that prevented the customers from using the product at all, or were problems with our product that were preventing the customer from executing their business.

Of course, I'm not saying that we didn't need to fix these things. But because we were only measuring severity, when I asked the engineers to look at fixing the installation, they would say with almost gleeful confidence, "Yes we have those issues logged into the system, and they are classified as level 17 bugs."

They could dutifully follow the official measures and avoid the work forever. I needed to get them to care.

So I arranged for three top engineers to each spend a week with the sales force. Their job was to shadow the sales engineers (the people who were responsible for installing and demoing the product). It was interesting that when I announced this program, the engineering response was enthusiastic, but they said, "The first thing we need to do is build a database!" When I asked for what purpose, they launched into a richly complex plan about being able to record and track feedback and learning from each customer visit. I said, "No, just go. The first step is not to build a database, it's to buy an airplane ticket."

So off they went. Of course, when they saw how difficult it was to get the product installed, and they saw the customers getting frustrated and angry, they became personally embarrassed at how terrible the initial user experience was. **Within two weeks of their return, all the install problems were fixed.**

I never needed to ask them to do it. It did not impact the schedule in any other way. The difference was that they cared personally, because they were embarrassed personally.

Later, to keep momentum in that direction, I still knew that "ease of use" for customers was not on the list of things engineers personally cared about. At this point, I needed to create momentum throughout the whole organization. So I came up with a goal that served as a more tangible control point. I said that one of the features of the next release was that it had to be "Fun in 15 minutes." This was a concept that every person, technical or not, could understand on a personal level. The goal was not simply to stop torturing customers, but to make the initial experience pleasant. I was initially greeted with a reaction that this was completely impossible.

I asked for some volunteers to lead a cross-functional brainstorming group that included people from engineering, sales, marketing, customer support, documentation, contracts, and delivery to define what "Fun in 15 minutes" would look like in a practical plan.

The result was a huge success. The limping cow was customer frustration with the failure to quickly achieve success. "Fun in 15 minutes" turned out to be an excellent control point measure, because for that to happen we needed to make changes not only to the technology itself, but to the packaging, the contracting and licensing, the customer support processes, the marketing approach, and other things. Many people and groups had to come together to make that happen. It was a good control point because when we achieved that outcome, it meant that all of the groups had achieved the right things. I never needed to measure all the details.

Pipeline Example: Control Point = Number of Successful Pilots

Here's another example of a control point. I worked with one company whose product was a point of sale technology for large retail establishments. The project had many moving parts of hardware and software development, marketing, supply chain management, sales partnerships, and so on. Reviewing the project detail would have put a respectable dent in the week (and my head).

This program had a revenue goal that was 18 months out. Meeting it meant the life or death of the program. They could track all the phase-review documents their hearts desired, but what we realized was the one thing that was the true measure of their ability to hit the revenue target was the number of successful customer pilots they could get by the six-month point. The team realized that the single greatest necessity and indicator of getting a deal closed was a successful pilot. That was the control point.

So they started to track the number of successful pilots each month. Because it took six months to convert a pilot into revenue, tracking all the project detail was not going to help them. But by targeting four new pilots right now, and four more each quarter, all the other stuff that needed to happen automatically got prioritized the right way because:

- If the pilots "were limping," they had to quickly fix whatever was blocking them.
- Sales teams and factory teams were all motivated to work together and prioritize the right stuff to get the pilots started and keep them working successfully.

It didn't matter whether the issue was sales, product, training, quality, support, some other issue, or a combination of these, because the one key control-point measure, the limping cow, was broken or stalled pilots. By choosing "successful pilot" as the control point, it facilitated a lot of the right behaviors across the whole organization. It worked as a control point because it meant that many different right things were happening, and they didn't need to measure them all individually.

Marketing Example: Control Point = Sales Reps Can Close a Deal Faster/Easier

One of the hardest things to measure in marketing is a brand awareness campaign. When I was a marketing leader, I always got into arguments with media salespeople about meaningful measures. Agencies would insist that I needed to advertise in ways that maximized "impressions" (how many people see your ad).

You feel like you have to measure something, so that's why marketing organizations and media companies join in this illusion to use impressions as a meaningful measure—to make each other feel better and give some sort of language to justify what they are doing. To me, impressions were always the wrong measure, because they were measuring a process step, not an observable outcome. If a gazillion people saw my ad, my impressions measure would say the campaign was wildly successful, but that has almost nothing to do with knowing whether that sighting caused any impact whatsoever. It wasn't a limping cow. It was a process step.

Finding the Control Point   First I defined the concrete desired outcomes of the awareness campaign. What would we *see*?

- More clients would know about us before we talk to them.
- More clients would prefer us over the competition before we talk to them.
- We would have fewer competitive battles.

I measured the observable outcome of an awareness campaign by creating a short survey for a group of salespeople in the region where the campaign was to run before it launched. It asked them things like:

- How often does a customer know about us when you first talk to them?
- How often do you have to defend us against a competitor they already know about?
- How often do they know and prefer us when you walk in the door?

Then I'd run the campaign.

Then six months later I'd ask those same questions again.

It was the outcome that mattered. If the awareness campaign worked, the sales reps got an easier start, less hassle, and more credibility when they walked in the door. They were happier! If nothing changed, I knew the campaign didn't work. How many people saw impressions of an ad was irrelevant. But if salespeople walk in now and say the customers have done their homework and have already seen our company as effective and credible, and we are preferred when the salesperson gets there, that is the important outcome.

The control point was: How many sales reps report that we are known and preferred when they walk in the door?

So to put it another way: When I looked for the limping cows, I was looking to reduce the number of limping salespeople!

CROSS-FUNCTIONAL MAGIC

So many organizations come to me with issues of silos and poor communication between functions.

In each of these examples, another important insight is that finding and measuring control points not only facilitates, but demands cross-functional communication and collaboration.

To achieve improvements in control points, whether they be for quality, pipeline, revenue, brand, or actual limping cows, it requires that multiple groups focus on the outcome and contribute their part—and that the parts are interconnected.

If you pick the right control point and make that what people are measured on, you will find that your teams will begin to work together because they have to—there is no other way forward. (See also Chapter 27: Sharing Information for more on improving cross-organization communication.)

IT'S OKAY IF IT'S HARD TO MEASURE

Sometimes this approach of looking for the limping cows and defining control points leads you to a metric that is an anecdotal vs. a hard measure. It's a mistake to dismiss an anecdotal measure because it is not a hard data measure. Control points by definition are a more broadly defined outcome than a detail or a process step. One of the reasons why we have so many bad measures is because details and process steps are so much easier to measure. But remember, they are bad measures—or at best, if they are necessary, they are not enough on their own.

If you've got a good control point defined, ask yourself what would the genuine measure of success be. If it turns out to be a description about how something is working, that's okay. Go with it.

NEXT

Another common thing that can halt execution during the Middle is an unclear, or uncommited resource plan. Are you being realistic about resources? Read on . . .

CHAPTER 5

Resource Reality

Your Strategy Is Where You Put Your Resources

You are on the hook! You know how important this new initiative is. Everyone knows how important this is! So you assume the right resource decisions are being made and implemented because if you don't complete the transformation, the whole organization is at risk. The new work must be getting the attention and resources that it requires because everyone has agreed that they are committed to moving the new strategy forward.

WHAT EVERYONE IS THINKING

Yikes! I've been asked to do this new stuff, but I still have all of my current workload, and I don't have more resources. So I can't move forward on the new stuff until I get some more resources.

Or . . .

This new stuff does not affect my team, so I'll just assume resources are being moved around elsewhere, and I'll keep my head down and keep doing my work. I'm not going to volunteer to give up resources from my team. I'll do everything I can to support the transformation; it's just that it doesn't involve me at this time.

RESOURCE REALITY

Another harsh reality during the "Middle" is that resources will never self-optimize to support a new initiative, strategy, or transformation.

Never. New stuff requires resources to do it. And very seldom does new stuff come with new, additive resources. So if you don't work through resource shifts out in the open, top-down, on purpose, they will not happen. Even if the organization as a whole has absorbed the importance of the strategy, no one will voluntarily give up resources to fund the new work.

You need to make sure that you have specifically resourced the activities necessary to achieve the outcomes you have put on your timeline. I realize that this sounds almost too basic to say, but I can't tell you how frequently I see organizations commit to plans without specifically applying the necessary resources to support those plans.

This happens often because resource discussions and decisions are hard. Really hard. It's tempting to avoid making hard choices, so those choices are delayed—and so before execution even starts, the strategy is at risk.

> **If there are no new resources to be added, the ability to do new stuff requires taking resources from old stuff. Simple. But difficult.**

As an example, I remember doing a strategy session with a client where they kept talking about their growth strategy for India and China. In the room was a woman I'll call B, who was heading this initiative. After about half of a day of talking about the importance of growth in India and China, among other business priorities, we got to the discussion about resources. To jump to the punchline, through forcing the discussion on resources I discovered that B (who had significant revenue assigned to her in the official business plan over the next two years) had no team and no budget. B was alone with no funding.

I said to the group, "In looking at your budget, it seems like your actual strategy is to have one person (B) investigate and write a plan for growth in India and China, not an actual strategy that should have revenue attached to it." They admitted that, in fact, they did not have a strategy that had revenue attached to it, and they changed their plan.

I see this all the time.

Your strategy is not what you say it is. Your strategy is where you put your resources.

Think about that. You can say whatever you want about what your strategy is, but if you want to know what your strategy actually is, just look at your budget. Remember, strategy is not what you talk about or hope for; it's about what you *do*. Your budget reflects what you are actually doing. Your budget tells the truth. Your budget describes what you will be doing, specifically throughout the Middle.

The problem is that getting clarity about where the resources come from causes conflict, and people tend to avoid conflict. But without assigning resources clearly to the new stuff, you'll never even start.

You need to work through the productive conflict and make the specific decisions about resources unambiguously clear. Resources will never self-optimize behind the scenes. You'll need to make tough decisions and hurt some people's projects (and feelings). Don't be fuzzy about how the new stuff will be resourced. The resource discussion and commitment will always be challenging and will always require clear, often painful decisions. I'll talk more about working through this type of resource conflict in the V = Valor section in Chapter 20: Clarity and Conflict.

REMEMBER, GREAT ISN'T CHEAP

Sticking with the idea that your strategy is what your budget says it is, one of the biggest mistakes I see business leaders at all levels make is to commit to a 100 percent plan on a less than 100 percent budget.

Here's how it starts. You have proven, maybe from your job interview, or your discussions or proposals, that you know exactly how to build or fix something to get the company to best in class in your area. So you'll have said: "Here is how I would improve the [quality, competitiveness, customer satisfaction, marketing effectiveness, service, sales performance, etc.]."

People are impressed because before you got there, they didn't even know what best in class looked like, and now they are really excited that there is someone who really knows what they are doing and can take them there. The company is expecting a huge transformation . . . but then without the right, realistic resource discussion the following can happen:

1. They expect you to deliver the dream scenario that you talked about.
2. They underestimate how far behind the company currently is and think it's not that big of a journey.
3. They don't give you enough budget to do it.

It's vitally important that, within the first moments of this discussion, you push back in a highly credible way so you are not set up to own an un-doable commitment.

Here is a great way to have this conversation.

Show the Scope of the Journey

One of the reasons that decision makers underestimate the resources required to get to a competitive position is because they do not fully realize the size of the hole they are in; or they don't fully understand why, or even that they are in a hole.

They know the company is not performing in your area as they wish, but because they do not have your expertise, they can't see the 37 reasons why. If you don't show them the depth of the hole you are in, they will expect to get to best in class right away *just because you showed up.*

If you don't show them the reality, there is a good chance they will believe that the only thing between the low point where they are now and best in class performance is you, with no additional staff, budget, or time to get there.

Don't let this happen. Act right away. Create something that looks like Figure 5.1. The vertical axis is whatever it takes to be competitive in your specific space.

Show the True Cost of Improving

You then need to give the management choices for different levels of outcomes and show that they cost different amounts. The conversation

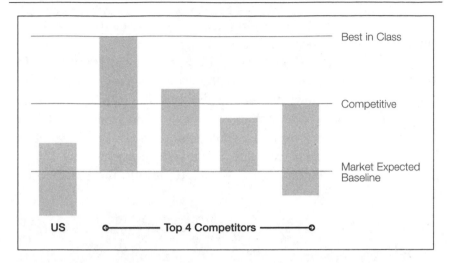

Figure 5.1   The Current State

you need to lead goes something like this: "OK, if you only increase my budget 10 percent, we can fix these three things, and add one item, but we can't add most of the competitive features. If that's the funding choice you make, this is what you will get."

The chart looks something like Figure 5.2.

> **You need to share the ownership of the problem with the decision makers. This is not your problem alone. This is a choice that the company needs to make.**

Plan	Budget	Staffing	Timeline
Fix the worst 2 problems that are killing us now	Similar budget as before I got here	No additional staff	Fixed within 6 months
Get to a less embarrassing baseline	10% more budget	Add 1 new hire	Fixed within 12 months
Get competitive in 2 key areas	50% more budget	Add 3 new hires	Fixed within 12 months
Get to best in class performance across the board	100% more budget	Add 2 new managers	Fixed within 18 months

Figure 5.2   Cost and Outcome Levels

Your job is to shine the spotlight on clearly defined choices, not to own all the risk of an un-doable strategy on your own.

Do yourself a favor and make sure you paint the resource reality clearly as soon as you can, and sign up for only as much as the funding allows. Share the knowledge of the scope of the journey. Share the decision about the level of investment and agree on expected outcomes throughout the Middle with the whole management team. It's not just you who should feel the pressure. Make sure everyone is sharing in the pressure to make the right resource trade-offs and has the same definition of success.

NEXT

But what if they don't give you the resources and tell you to do it anyway? Read on . . .

CHAPTER 6

Don't Sign Up for the Impossible

WHAT IF THEY TELL YOU TO "DO IT ANYWAY"?

In some cases, the approach I described in the last chapter to outline the choices between okay, good, and great and to share the problem of choosing the investment level does not work. You've articulated the choices and investment levels, and then the powers that be say, "You are not getting the funding, but do the whole thing anyway."

In your heart you know it can't be done, but they are being unwaveringly insistent; and you are afraid that you will get fired if you tell the truth and say, "This can't be done without additional resources."

Caveat: Generally, It's Really Important to Be Self-Funding

There is a little bit of a slippery slope here because executives do look for leaders who can do things that others say are impossible—leaders that can do great things without demanding more resources all the time. The best business leaders (at every level) do not rely on getting more money every year to do new things. It's great if you can get new money, but if you can't, that doesn't mean you can't do new things.

What I'm talking about is not just piling more work on your team. It means conducting your business in such a way that you choose to stop doing some things each year, *and* that you find ways to get the same stuff done for less cost next year. You should always be looking for ways to increase your efficiency and reduce your expenses, so that you can re-invest the savings in where the business needs to go. You should be reducing costs every year on the current work and freeing up resources for new things and improvements—without being asked to do so.

But . . . You Still Can't Do the Impossible

There is a vital difference between an aggressive stretch plan and a total impossibility.

I'm all for stretching. I'm all for proactively finding resources to do things from within your own budget, so you don't always ask for new resources to do new things. But when you know, because you have studied every angle and squeezed every last bit of cost out already, that what you are being asked to do is totally impossible, then you need to make a choice. Tell the truth, or proceed on a plan you don't believe in.

What Everyone Is Thinking

This is impossible. This is so screwed up!

Never underestimate the ability of the people doing the work to know if a strategy is sound or not. When a strategy is realistic and supported by resources, people can feel that. When a strategy is an exciting mission to take a new hill and everyone has to stretch, people can get motivated by that. But when a strategy is impossible, and the resources and timelines do not match the delivery goals and revenue expectations at all, you are never hiding that from the people doing the work. They can see it (maybe even more clearly than you).

If you embark on this path, the credibility of the management will plummet and morale will be terrible—because no one has the resources to do anything well, and the goals simply can't be met. You are asking people to continue working aboard a sinking ship. They will be looking for a lifeboat or an island to hop onto.

This Can't Be Done

Sometimes you will be asked to deliver the impossible, and you will need a strategy to push back with credibility.

A common version of this happens when a business leader is given "a number" they need to make. It doesn't matter what the actual realistic, achievable revenue number is, the conversation starts and ends with, "We need the revenue to be this number." I have seen months of planning be thrown out and literally overwritten in a moment, when someone with the power of the pen changes a single cell on the spreadsheet for "revenue target" with no explanation.

This might happen because:

1. The CEO promised that amount of revenue to the board and investors, and he will lose his job if it is not achieved.
2. This number needs to be plugged into the plan of a bigger business unit who has made a non-negotiable commitment to the company or board.
3. Because (this is the most common reason for this false revenue number) the revenue is required to support the current expenses of the business.

I can tell you that in my own career, I have never succumbed to this pressure. I could never sign up for a plan that I knew I could not deliver. I have led several turnarounds and transformations, and there was always a moment when I told the truth about what the new thing could be, when I knew that what I was telling the executive committee was something they did not want to hear:

The business you want does not exist.
What I am offering is to give you a smaller, good business that functions and that is profitable.
It is not as big as you want it to be, but at least it is real.
I won't sign up for a bigger number that is not doable.

At this point I have experienced one of two reactions. One was, "Thank you, you are the first one to tell us the truth. We don't like it but your plan is doable, please proceed." The other one was, "This is not good enough. If you can't deliver what we need, we'll get someone else who can."

Any time the latter happened I said, "I'm okay with that. I'm sure you can find someone who will commit to whatever you want, but I doubt they will deliver it. It's your choice. If you'd like me to lead this, I will actually deliver this smaller plan."

I've never lost a job over this. I see no upside to making a commitment that is not real.

Turtles All the Way Down

Whenever I see this tendency to build a plan on a false number, or a false premise, I always think about a story I have heard that has been attributed to many different sources all over the world. Here is one version I got on Wikipedia:

> After a lecture on cosmology and the structure of the solar system, William James* was accosted by a little old lady.
>
> "Your theory that the sun is the center of the solar system, and the earth is a ball which rotates around it, has a very convincing ring to it, Mr. James, but it's wrong. I've got a better theory," said the little old lady.
>
> "And what is that, madam?" inquired James politely.
>
> "That we live on a crust of earth which is on the back of a giant turtle."
>
> Not wishing to demolish this absurd little theory by bringing to bear the masses of scientific evidence he had at his command, James decided to gently dissuade his opponent by making her see some of the inadequacies of her position.
>
> "If your theory is correct, madam," he asked, "what does this turtle stand on?"
>
> "You're a very clever man, Mr. James, and that's a very good question," replied the little old lady, "but I have an answer to it. And it is this: The first turtle stands on the back of a second, far larger, turtle, who stands directly under him."
>
> "But what does this second turtle stand on?" persisted James patiently.

---

* In John R. Ross's 1967 linguistics dissertation, "Constraints on Variables in Syntax," the scientist is identified as the Harvard psychologist and philosopher, William James.

To this the little old lady crowed triumphantly. "It's no use, Mr. James—it's turtles all the way down."

I see this play out in business over and over again. **But it's not turtles that are providing the support for holding up the business; it's the false revenue number.**

The whole plan—the strategy, the staff, the investments—are all based on a false revenue number. I think of this story every time I see a business leader or team sign up for a plan for which there is no factual basis to support that revenue target. But they have a crumb of a reason to create this story, so they stick to it. And then they build bigger and bigger business cases on top of the unsubstantiated premise—it's turtles all the way down.

Sure you can base the number on the something, and come up with some story why that number is a good number, but if you dig too much and look for the real support, you're not going to find it. You're only going to find hopeful distractions to make everyone feel like the number is real even though it isn't. (It's just the next turtle.)

I simply couldn't live with the "turtles all the way down" method of planning. So I refused to put myself in that position. But what that also implied was that to pursue a realistic revenue number, I had to follow through on getting the expense plan in shape, which was always painful.

Pick the Right Revenue and Expense Target

As I mentioned previously, the most common reason for having a revenue target that is too high is to support the current, too-high expense base.

The most pivotal decisions you can make in the business are based on this: What are your revenue and expense targets? If you are building a company and are in investment mode, there is a little more play here, based on the appetite of the market and the patience of your investors. But in a going business, if you get this wrong, you can get it really wrong.

When companies try to support an artificially high, unsupportable expense target, they can't do anything well.

When the expenses are too high, and the revenue is not supporting that level of expense, then budgets get squeezed and no one has enough resources for anything. You can't make any investments. You are always doing a lesser job than you want because no one can afford to do anything the right way.

Every single day, every single person comes to work feeling like they are failing and that you are all collectively failing. Every week there is another "no" to a request for needed resources. Every month there is a panic when you don't make the numbers, and then there are hours of soul-destroying meetings to analyze what happened, and why the revenue was not higher.

So then to be responsible, more programs are squeezed, more projects are delayed. Either directly or as a byproduct, more talented people go away, and the people who remain continue to suffer, fighting their battles with too few resources and knowing in their hearts that you won't make the revenue plan next month either (because it's turtles all the way down).

The answer here is structurally very simple: **Cut the expenses to a level that the actual revenue plan will support. Get healthy, then grow from there.**

It may seem that I have a pretty harsh view of this. But it's because I have been through it so many times, and each and every time *everything* was better afterwards. Everyone comes to work feeling like they can succeed. The projects that remain are well funded—they can succeed. You hit the revenue plan for the month. Then instead of spending half your time agonizing over why you didn't meet the revenue plan, everyone spends that time moving the business even further forward—because they can. People are motivated.

The pain of sizing the expenses correctly is a one-time thing that affects some of the people. The pain of having expenses too high for the actual, achievable revenue goal is painful for every single person, every single day forever after—and puts the whole business at risk. Everyone suffers. I'm not a fan of layoffs. It should always be the very last resort. It's a great thing to create and keep jobs and it's a terrible thing to lay people off. But—it doesn't help anyone to be in a failing business, whose effective business model is "turtles all the way down." It's unsustainable. If you maintain this, at some point instead of some people losing their jobs, everyone loses their jobs.

DO WHAT YOU CAN

When I was running a global marketing organization for a computer business, the new management team of which I was a part inherited a turnaround situation to run a business whose realistic revenue plan was less than half of the committed revenue plan. The current expenses matched the high revenue number, of course. I was responsible for creating a winning strategy, but as part of that strategy we needed to reduce the revenue plan by more than a factor of two. And we needed to reduce expenses to be inline. To implement the new plan, I needed to cut my annual budget from $140M to $60M. This was not a small change! It required a total reinvention. It was very painful. But we got around the corner.

> **Within the first year we took that business from losing $50M every quarter to making $50M in the first year. The pain was gone. It was replaced by focused action, and pride and hope.**

One of the things I see so many companies struggle with is the thinking that if you cut too deep, the business will stop and fail—that it will be impossible to be in business with so many fewer people and resources. It feels like there is absolutely no way to be successful after so deep a cut.

I was grateful to have learned this lesson very early in my career when I was in a start-up company that had at its peak about 60 people. I was the product marketing manager in a group of five marketing people reporting to a vice president of marketing. One week I left on a business trip, and by the time I got back the company had been downsized to 30 people and I had a new job—as the marketing department! It was just me. I did not think I could succeed, but more importantly than that, I didn't think the company could succeed with this deep of a cut. After the layoff, we lost about five more of our top engineers. It really felt impossible. What could we do with so few people and without so many of our core product development people?

What Could We Do? We Did What We Could

What happened? We did what we could. We picked a smaller strategy and we did it well. We made it to break even.

That experience gave me the confidence that reducing expenses not only doesn't kill the company, but when you size the expenses for the realistic revenue, and fund the few things that you can do well, you can succeed. This same dynamic played out in my work with transformations of large organizations too. Get your organization and expenses sized to reflect a realistic, doable plan—plot your course through the Middle based on what you can actually do, and then do it.

This lesson of finding the new, smaller, successful plan was the inspiration of a phrase I coined and used many times over: "Do Less with Less." **I hate the adage of "Do More with Less." It doesn't work, and it makes everyone feel worse. But "Do Less with Less"— people can really get behind that!**

SOMETHING MUST GET MORE MONEY

Here is one more big lesson on resources.

If you have a strategy that involves cutting costs, the simple, first test of "is this a good strategy or not?" is to make sure that while you are cutting, no matter how deep, that there are some things that are getting more money than before.

> **If in a cut nothing is getting more money than before (at least proportionally), you are just running a smaller version of the same struggling business that is trying to do too many things.**

Everyone can know it and can feel it if the plan makes sense, and if it is doable. And they also know it and can feel it when the plan is based on "turtles all the way down."

NEXT

Before leaving the Middle, it's important to make sure that you have a support structure in place, personally. Transformations are tricky business. How will you reduce your personal risk in driving your transformation?

Read on . . .

CHAPTER 7

Sponsors and Enemies

Reduce Your Personal Risk

SUPPORT AND SABOTAGE

Before we go in to the rest of the model, it's important to make sure that another thing you are very clear about through the long "middle" is your support and sponsorship—and possible enemies.

Yes, you need your team to be ready, motivated, and capable to move your transformation forward, but you also need to be aware that without sponsorship, your transformation could die an unnatural and painful death at the hands of others who don't want you to succeed.

I have seen this happen to leaders too many times, and it is a real shame. Here's how it plays out. The leader is brilliant, well liked, and generally well respected. They launch a new strategy or transformation initiative, which they are personally very excited about and invested in. They get their team on board. But then they make the mistake of thinking that only their organization needs to stay informed and involved.

Without the right broad support in place for your transformation above and around your organization, if another group raises an objection, and the executive management has been out of the loop on what you are doing—you will be at risk.

Am I the only one who cares about this?

That is the question. Make sure you are never the only one who cares. Always ask yourself, "Who else cares about this?" If there is no one at an equal or higher level than you who *actively* cares about what you are doing, there is too much risk. One of the ugly challenges you need to face through the whole Middle is that people from anywhere can decide to try to sabotage you and/or your strategy. If you fail to build the right kind of sponsorship along the way, your strategy and your career are exposed to enormous risk. I see two common issues.

1. I Don't Have Time to be Self-Promoting

Some leaders are comfortable building bridges and securing sponsorship, and others are not. I've worked with executives who see no value in communicating outside their organization at all. They think it's a political game, without value, and even somehow morally wrong to focus on communicating instead of working. But they'll say, "I don't want to waste time." In my book *RISE*, I talked about the need to *connect* better and the fact that successful people are the ones who have the most support. This is even more true if you are leading an important transformation.

When I watch the careers of these communication-avoiders progress, well . . . they don't progress.

They try to stay on the high ground and say, "I don't play politics. I believe that my results will speak for themselves." To me, this is never about politics. It's about effectiveness. And it's about insurance. And it's about the harsh reality that your results seldom ever speak for themselves without some shepherding of the communication about them from you.

> **If you don't invest the time and effort to build sponsorship, as soon as your initiative gets attacked, you by definition are personally under attack because there is no one standing with you.**

In that moment you will not have high credibility because *your* strategy, what *you alone* are doing, is called into question. At that point the powers that be will be looking for others to validate your strategy. If there is no one eagerly stepping up to validate what you are doing—you lose.

If you continue to believe that it's not important to communicate, build support, and gain sponsorship, and therefore not secure sponsorship, you will not come out on top in a disagreement or a restructuring.

I recommend a change in thinking to "I must create sponsors" instead of "I don't want to be self-promoting" or "I don't have time."

2. I Believe Everyone Still Supports My Strategy

The other situation I see is that a leader will be brought in to drive a transformation, and they initially are on a great path to lead a wonderful improvement in the business. They assume that their peers, all the executives, and the board of directors are supporting the transformation because that is what they were hired to do, and in the beginning that might have even been true.

But once they get into the Middle, they don't continue to provide updates and actively recruit sponsors for their work among these other groups above and around them. They focus solely on their team and their transformation—which feels sensible because in itself it's a huge job. They got the green light at the beginning, so there is no need to keep getting approval.

Sadly, this thinking is wrong. I have seen executives who are doing a great job leading a transformation that they were hired to do, but there are factions who do not like it. If these factions (usually long-time incumbents who hate change) have more sponsorship (old relationships) than the busy new executive, the dissenters start to become very powerful.

Again, if you don't invest in sponsorship along the way, because you think you already have it, you will put your initiative and your career at grave risk. The Middle offers a long time for saboteurs and enemies to undermine you. Sponsorship requires care and feeding throughout the whole Middle.

This is particularly important if you are the leader of a cross-organization transformation, and it's your job to get a bunch of business units to cooperate to accomplish a centralized mission. Without true sponsorship, you run the risk of spending years groveling with each business unit, each of which might say they support the transformation, but has the power to ignore you if you don't have a high level sponsor insisting that each business unit applies budget and energy to the transformation. Without a real sponsor, after a couple of years you will end up with a reputation for annoying everyone, and failing to deliver the transformation. Don't let this happen to you!

ACHIEVING SPONSORSHIP

What sponsorship looks like is that you have a few people above and around you in the organization who truly care about what you are doing and who are personally invested in your success. I have found that the best way to do this is to build relationships with a handful of key influencers, treat some of them like mentors, and treat some of them like project sponsors.

With the mentors, keep them in the loop about what you are experiencing, what people are saying, and what dissenters are complaining about. Ask them if they have any advice on how to continue to build alignment.

With the sponsors, keep them in the loop about timelines, milestones, decisions, and external partner or customer feedback on the validity of your transformation. Ask them to help.

To secure real sponsorship: give your sponsor a job.

The most powerful thing you can do to secure real sponsorship is to give your sponsor a job to do. Involve them in a real way. Sponsors in name only are not actually sponsors. If you want their hearts to be in it, ask them to do stuff for you. Ask them to join the kick-off meeting. Ask them to get on the phone once a month for 5 to 10 minutes at the beginning or end of your team meetings. You can script things you need them to say. Ask for their help on securing funding or to be the tiebreaker in a decision. The more things you can get them personally involved in, the more they will be engaged and loyal to your initiative.

Then if your transformation or initiative comes into question or is under attack from a saboteur, they will be personally motivated to stand up for the program because it is their program too. You can't get there (all the way through the Middle) without support and sponsors.

Next: O = Organization

You also need to be very truthful about your organization and their capability to do what you need them to do. Going forward with the wrong team is a formula for disaster. How will you make sure you've got the right people helping you?

Read on . . .

PART 2

O = Organization

Are You Leading the Team You Have or the Team You Need?

There is no effective antidote for the wrong team.

Transformation is hard. You need help. You can't afford to have anyone on your team who is not fully on board: ready, able, and motivated to MOVE forward. You need a strategy to create the right organizational structure and to get the right people in the right roles.

CHAPTER **8**

The Right Team

The Fundamental Ingredient for a Highly Effective Team

Y ou are facing the very beginning of a necessary transformation. You are thinking through all the new things that need to be done. There will be things that need to be started, stopped, fixed, invented, re-designed, re-negotiated . . . and, as you are cataloging all the new stuff in your mind, you think about your team—your current team. In these first moments of a transformation you still have the same, existing organization. You ask yourself, "Is this the right team?"

In your heart you secretly know that not everyone on your current team is the best choice to succeed in the new mission. But it's really hard to make a change, and you probably still need them to keep working on the current plans. And you might also be feeling bad and insecure, thinking, *I like these people. I brought these people in initially! Who am I to now tell them that they are not going to be part of the new business strategy? Maybe I'll just move forward with my existing team, and they will be able to evolve to be capable enough in their new jobs. Or maybe I really do need to change the team. I don't know. This is hard!*

WHAT EVERYONE IS THINKING

This new strategy is kind of scary. I'd like to feel more confident that the leadership team is really competent enough to lead us. There are some leaders in this business that seem really smart, but others that seem in over their heads. I'm not sure they all agree on what is important—that makes me a little nervous! When I hear about all this new stuff we are supposed to do, I'm not sure we have the skills here to do it. I think there is organization change coming. What happens to my job?

It's worth noting that you are not hiding a bad organization structure or weak leaders from the rest of your team. Nor are you hiding a need or intention to re-structure. They can see it. Your best approach here is when you do make a change, to get it really right so that the new organization makes sense to everyone.

THERE IS NO EFFECTIVE ANTIDOTE FOR THE WRONG TEAM

There is no more important thing you can do as a business leader than to build the right team. Every time I hated my job, or felt like I was drowning or failing, a mentor would tell me, "Patty, you need to build the right team."

Every time I was in a new management position, I built a new management team. And every time, before I had the new team in place, I suffered. It was not that the individuals were particularly bad in some way. It was that the team as a whole was the wrong team to accomplish what the business needed to get done. As long as I had the old team, doing the new stuff proved virtually impossible. And I had to shoulder all the weight of thinking about the new stuff by myself.

> **If you find yourself working overly hard because there are too many things that you can't delegate to anyone—you have the wrong team.**

A Team That Is Ready to Move

As a business leader I can remember the feeling so clearly at the moment when I finally got the right team in place. It was always a little scary to get there, but those moments always held a combination of relief and excitement for me because I knew the big pain was ending. I felt less scared and more certain, and even excited, about the future. My confidence that we could actually achieve what we needed to do soared. I could go home for the first time in a long while and sleep well. It was such a wonderful thing. With the right team, not only could we move forward . . . it was more like we couldn't *not* move forward. The team was ready and raring to go.

With the right team, you can take on any challenge, and most of your energy is focused on actually moving forward.

With the wrong team, you work too hard—for not enough return. You get frustrated and tired. As a leader you need to spend too much of your time and energy compensating for the fact that you don't have the right team.

Making changes to your team is never easy to do. There is always angst and controversy and risk in getting there. But it is always worth it.

A Lesson from the Dogs

A while back I had a chance to go dogsledding in Canada. It was fun. I highly recommend it if you ever get the chance. At the beginning of the day there were 17 sled-dog teams lined up on the sides of the path. There was a 30-minute briefing that we listened to while standing outside in 36 degrees below! The dogs were in their harnesses, mostly lying and lounging in the snow. All the sleds had their brakes on. (The brake is basically a stake that is driven into the snow so the sled can't move.)

When the dogs knew that the 30 minute briefing was ending (they had heard this briefing before), without any cue from the guides, they all jumped up, pointed forward, and were ready to *go*. They had such motivation and energy that you could see and feel it. And because the sleds had their brakes on, there was tremendous energy and tension in the ropes. **All the ropes were tight.**

At that moment I felt such a wave of purpose and energy. It was palpable. Every dog was pointing forward and ready, willing, and anxious to *go*. All you needed to do was release the brake.

I remember thinking, *I have felt this same energy when I finally was able to build the right team, and we reached that moment where we were all committed to go forward.* This has become my metaphor, and my test, for the right team: When you look at your team, you need to ask yourself, honestly, "Are all the ropes tight?"

And if all the ropes are *not* tight, your job is *not* to try and go forward with the wrong team; it's to create a team where in fact, all the ropes are tight—that's the fundamental ingredient of a successful team. Here are some rope-tightening questions you can ask yourself:

1. **Are all your team members facing forward?**

    This may seem like a simple question, but more often than not, there is at least one person who is simply not facing forward along with the rest of the team. They may be facing sideways (confused about where you are going) or backwards (in disagreement with where you are going). They may be sticking to an old way of doing things, or refusing to change their point of view on something important.

    For example, say you've committed to a new manufacturing process that requires a fundamental change to your infrastructure. This one person is very invested in the old infrastructure and disagrees with the change. So every time the new work comes anywhere near him, all the decisions, tasks, and communications about the new way stall. Instead of investing to help make the new way possible, this person keeps advocating for the old way and shooting holes in the new way.

    Instead of helping to overcome the problems involved in making the new way succeed, he is highlighting the problems and saying why it won't work, or he is ignoring the problems so they will never get solved. Everyone else is trying to run forward. This person's rope may be tight, but it's pulling in the wrong direction!

2. **Is everyone on your team truly in alignment about what the course is and what their role is?**

    Can everyone on the team run forward without getting tangled up? Or are there points of disagreement or confusion that need to be resolved? If people's roles aren't clear, or if you have competing, conflicting, or duplicate efforts within your organization, the ropes will get tangled up. When you say "go," everyone may start running, but not in the same direction. They don't all see the same curves in the road ahead. The mission looks different to each of them. You may still be able to move forward, but you lose a lot of time and energy sorting out questions and issues that would be eliminated if everyone on the team had a clear view and a clean charter. If you fail to create clarity of purpose and roles, the ropes will become tangled, and energy that could have been spent moving forward will get re-directed and lost in the tangles.

3. **Is each person capable and up to the task required of their role?**

Can every person on your team pull their share of the weight—truly? Do they fully have the ability, the judgment, and the communication and leadership skills to do the job that needs to be done? And are they willing and motivated to do their part?

When there is a team member who can not pull their share of the weight, if they remain on the team, the manager and other team members are forced to compensate. And every time someone needs to compensate for a weak team member, there is a person not doing what they should be doing. Progress slows. You have a dog that just can't (or won't) run fast enough to keep up. If they are not helping to pull the sled, there is no tension on their rope. In the worst case you will need to get off the sled and go up front and help pull. You may enjoy pulling the sled sometimes, but just remember: First, you should be steering; second, you are paying someone to not do their job; third, the other team members will wonder why they are pulling so much of the weight.

4. **Are they all motivated to go where they need to go?**

This is as important as any of the other questions. Do all the members of your team personally care about where you need to go? Are they engaged? Are they invested? There are some people who go through the motions of facing forward, and they have enough capability to run just fast enough so that their rope doesn't visibly droop. They put on a great show of their effort, but they are only just barely pulling their share of the load. These are the people who enjoy the lifestyle of having this job, but don't really want to run all that hard or pull any extra heavy weight or go uphill. Or these are the team members who give weak or passive aggressive support. To look at them, the effort looks right, but if you are honest about it, they are really not helping as much as someone who could be in that role truly pulling for the team's success.

Just Remove the Brake!

I've had all of these issues on the teams I inherited whenever I started a new job. That's why, when 17 sled-dog teams jumped up before even being told to go, and all the ropes were tight, in that moment I thought, *Ah*, that's *the team you need! Everyone is pulling their weight in the same direction—ready, willing, and anxious to* go. *All I have to do is remove the brake.*

ARE ALL OF YOUR MANAGERS GOOD MANAGERS?

Before leaving the topic of all the ropes being tight, another foundational question you need to ask yourself is this: Are all the managers in my organization good managers?

Many organizations settle for having people in managerial roles, who quite simply are not good managers. Some common causes for this are that people have been promoted because they excelled at doing their job function, or simply because there was a need for another manager to reduce the span of control, so they just named an individual to lead part of the team. Selections are sometimes made in ways that seem as though it doesn't matter. It matters! It is one of the things that matters most.

> **One of the biggest things you can do to impact your business growth and bottom line is to insist that every manager is a good manager.**

People who are not suited to management wreak havoc. I know this firsthand because I regularly interact with first- and mid-level managers from companies in many industries all over the world who ask for help with how to deal with a bad manager. On my membership Coaching Hour calls that are part of my FORWARD program for professional development, I hear so many stories of bad managers: poor (sometimes back-stabbing) communication, lack of decision making, lack of accountability, lack of support, poor planning and resource management, prevention of opportunities for development and visibility, lack of ability to understand and make trade-offs, can't stick to a long-term plan in favor of shiny objects, politically motivated, inaccessible . . . this list goes on and on. There are a lot of bad managers out there. It will serve you well to make sure that you select, support, train, and set expectations about what is required of a good manager in your organization.

With bad managers lurking about in your organization, people who should be doing work are instead getting confused, discouraged, frustrated, and scared. Bad managers are preventing them from doing the right things for the business, so your strategy stalls.

You need your managers to be engaging, motivating, supporting, and facilitating the right work, not preventing it.

This is one of my favorite types of work to do with corporations— to train their managers to be good managers—because it makes such a huge difference not only to the business, but to the health and sanity of everyone involved!

In one of the monthly webinars in my FORWARD program, I shared a simple test: *Are you a good manager?* I'll share it with you here. Every good manager should be able to get a *yes* answer from each of their employees on the following questions:

- Do you understand the strategy of our business?
- Do you understand the mission of your team and why it is important?
- Do you understand how your job fits into that mission?
- Are your strengths acknowledged? Do you get to use your strengths in your work?
- Do you know what is expected of you? Do you know how you will be measured? Did you have input into this process?
- Do you feel acknowledged and recognized by your manager?
- Do you feel informed and in the loop about information that is relevant to you and your work?
- Do you feel like you can work without fear?

- Do you feel like you can deliver agreed outcomes without being micromanaged?
- Do you feel like you can give your manager feedback without fear?
- Are you excited about something you are working on?

NOTE TO LEADERS MAKING CHANGES: ARE YOU LEADING THE TEAM YOU HAVE OR THE TEAM YOU NEED?

One of the tough things about a business transformation is that when you initially sign up to do something different, in that moment you still have the same people. Usually the new thing is bigger, more sophisticated, or more challenging in some way. One of the ways I see organizations get stuck is that they try to do the new stuff with the same people. Not everyone will be capable of what the new way requires. Not everyone will be able to step up. Do a really honest assessment: "Are all the ropes tight?"

NOTE TO EVERYONE WHOSE JOB MAY CHANGE: WHAT HAPPENS TO YOUR ROLE NOW?

Of course, organizational changes can be stressful and difficult if not outright scary. If you face the risk of losing your job, it feels terrible!

Awareness is really important here. First, be aware that the new strategy will likely resort in some changes in personnel. Don't be surprised by this. Understand the strategy. Don't hide your head in the sand and just wait. Assess your situation and that of your team. Educate yourself as much as possible about the new goals of the business. Be ready to engage in planning and discussion. You might not always feel like you are being told all the answers along the way, but be as ready and educated as you can when you get the opportunity to have an opinion.

It's important to realize that it's not a good personal strategy to dig in and attempt to preserve your job and team exactly as it exists today as the new change rolls out. It's a much better strategy, both from a business and personal perspective, to make a sincere effort to understand the changes at hand, and to be proactively ready to tune your job if necessary to better support where the business is going.

Don't wait to be asked or told. Think about it. The personal leadership that is required here is to conceive of and recommend changes if they are necessary instead of just waiting for others to make all the decisions.

I can tell you that every time this happened to me, my willingness to proactively say something helpful was always appreciated and rewarded. For example: "As I understand the new strategy and the way that the new organization is shaping up, it seems that my role is no longer needed. Here is an idea for how I can change the focus of my team to support this critical part of the new strategy. I can continue to lead the team, but I think it would be okay to combine my team with this other organization. Then I could work on this other new thing that is really critical . . ."

If it turns out that your job will be eliminated because of the new strategy, your helpful, proactive, positive leadership behaviors are the best way to find your way into another opportunity in the new structure, and to help your team members land well. (Also read my book *RISE* to learn how to make sure that you have built a foundation of positive visibility and support for your career.)

Consider your role and your goals in the new organization, or in the same organization with the new strategy if the organization does not change, as you read through the next chapters in Part 2 (O = Organization). Think seriously about optimizing your organization, too. These chapters will give you the tools to proactively build the strongest team possible and develop your own leadership abilities.

NEXT: DREAM BIG

What is the ideal organization to accomplish your objectives? Don't settle for the organization structure you have if it's not the right one. Build the one you need. Build the team that will be in the strongest position to *move* the business forward. Read on . . .

CHAPTER 9

Organize for Outcomes

Create the Ideal, Blank-Sheet Org Chart

You've come to terms with the fact that your existing organization structure is not the right one for the future.

You've decided to make some changes. So you take out a copy of your org chart and start thinking about moving people around, choosing your strong performers and worrying about others. You need to think about scaling but are not certain that everyone on your team can scale. You can't quite figure out how to have the conversation with them, because they each probably think that they can scale. They would not want to report to someone new or get pushed down a level. They will react badly if they don't continue to report to you. Then you start to worry that there may be other people on your team who no longer have a role at all in the new structure. You might need to hire for one or two new positions, but you're not sure you'll be able to get the approval for a new hire. This is so stressful!

WHAT IS THE BUSINESS MOTIVATION FOR ORGANIZATIONAL CHANGE?

Take a deep breath. Organization change is never easy. It makes everyone nervous, including the leader who is making the change!

Often, leaders make the mistake of thinking about organization changes in terms of moving the existing people around. A better approach, when you are at these crossroads and you need to make a change, is to first focus on the business outcome, and then decide what the ideal organization would be to achieve that business outcome. It's easy to get paralyzed when you start your thinking about the people who are already there and what they will think. So don't start there. Start with a blank sheet.

Remember, an org chart is never about the people. It's about what needs to get done.

The job of a manager at any level is not to form a new organization by simply moving around the people you already have. Your job as a leader is to develop, and if necessary, change the people to build a highly capable team that can do what the business needs in the future.

In my career there was one instance in particular when I needed to do a major reorganization, and I was really scared that I was going to lose everyone in the process. But at the same time I realized that not doing the re-org was not an option either.

One of the reasons this was scary was that most external observers thought the business was doing great. But I quickly realized it was resting on its past successes, and in fact, while it was indeed growing and profitable, it was growing slower than the market. And there were plenty of competitors with fresher products who were moving faster. This was not a good trajectory. *Conclusion #1: From an external pressure perspective, we needed a transformation.*

Then when I looked inside the business, the picture got even worse. The business unit had been set up to be about eight separate business units going to market in parallel. We had duplicate and conflicting efforts everywhere. And we did not have a single person focused on important things that needed to happen in between and across all these business units to build a clear and differentiated offer for the changing market. These gaps became very clear when I started having executive staff meetings, and each time I put the biggest problems on the table for discussion—failing partner channel, unsupported sales force, lack of consistent marketing message, lack of product integration—everybody just looked at each other. No one officially owned solving any of these business-wide problems.

Hmmm . . . nobody at the table owned fixing any of the biggest issues. Note to self: wrong organization structure!

Also, within the first couple of months, we had two big customer and partner events, one in Europe and one in the United States. At these events pretty much everyone yelled at me. Channel partners would get me in a corner at the cocktail party and tell me, "We don't know what to sell, we have one of your business units telling us to sell one thing, and then another business unit telling us to sell something totally different instead. Your products are competing with one another. I don't understand your product line. You seem to have three different products for one thing and five ways to do another." I remember at one particular event, someone on my staff actually snuck me out the back way after about four hours of this at a dinner (where I got no dinner), so that I could get out alive.

The next week at the U.S. event, I heard two salespeople talking and one of them said (one of the worst possible things you can hear one of your sales reps say), "I've got customers with budget to spend right now, but I don't know what I'm supposed to sell them." [Heavy sigh] *Conclusion #2: From an internal perspective, we needed a transformation.*

THE IDEAL, BLANK-SHEET ORG CHART

So I started with a blank sheet of paper, and first focused on the business outcome: I needed a single market leading product strategy; a single, super-compelling marketing message that was not confusing; and a consistent go to market approach for the sales force and the channel partners.

Using the blank-sheet approach, I decided that I was going to reorganize the business into a single business unit, with a leader for each functional area. That organization structure was not perfect either (no structure is ever perfect), but it solved more problems than it caused, and it solved the burning problems I had at the time. It matched the business outcome of having a single, integrated strategy by eliminating individual business units that were competing against each other, and by forming one team that could present the unified strategy to the partners and customers. It solved the problem of getting owners for all the biggest issues we were facing, which in the current structure had no owners. It was an organization structure that was designed to deliver what the business needed.

Here is the process I use for developing an ideal, blank-sheet org chart:

1. **Start with the desired outcome for the business.**

   Start by thinking about what needs to get done. Get really clear about what business outcomes you need to deliver. Really understand and articulate the specific work, strategic problem solving, concrete outcomes, and control points that your team needs to drive. Put them on a timeline to make it tangible through the Middle.

2. **Next, draw your ideal blank-sheet org chart.**

   Start with a blank sheet of paper. Really start fresh. Don't even look at your current org chart. Don't just rework the current roles or try to place the people you already have on the team in new boxes. Just think about what the business really needs and what outcomes you are on the hook for. Then draw a picture of what the ideal team to deliver that would be. Think through what the specific roles (roles, not people) on your new team would need to be to drive the key business outcomes— not just now but in the future. It can be a very liberating and inspiring experience to start with a blank sheet of paper and draw a picture of your ideal team with no names at all in the boxes.

3. **Now, clearly define each specific *new* role. Really work to articulate the new stuff that is different. This is the key.**

   It's very important to define every role as a *new* role. Even if the function is the same in the old and new world, for example: Product Management. You need to make it really clear that it is not the same job as it used to be. You need to define what is new and different about the product management role in the new world. Add things like the ability to drive innovation, or to influence adversaries, implement new technologies, be highly credible at executive level communications, or to personally transform business, partner, or sales models.

   Once you define the new org and the new roles, you have just created a clear and actionable picture of your goal.

4. **Get input.**

You most likely have one or two trusted people on your staff who you are confident will fit into the new structure. Share your blank-sheet structure with them. Get their reactions and inputs. I have almost always tuned my ideal blank-sheet thinking after discussing it with some of my trusted team members. The added benefit here is that if you bring some team members into the design of the new organization, they will be much more ready to support the new structure moving forward.

Also, at this point I think it is very important to talk to people at all levels of the organization. You don't need to reveal your whole organization design, but if you have a lot of conversations to get people's opinions at all levels about what is working and not working, you will get a lot smarter *and* you will build trust. By having these conversations more broadly, by the time you roll out your new organization, people at all levels will be saying, "That makes sense," and they will see their fingerprints on it. You'll learn more about the value of engaging the broader audience early on in Part 4 (E = Everyone).

The Hard Part

Okay. Now, if you had the perfect person in each of those boxes, life would be great.

So, now comes the hard part. It is likely that all the people on your current team do not fit exactly into this ideal structure. Two things will become clear at this point:

1. Some of your current people will obviously map into the new roles. Put them there.

2. You will most likely end up with both some empty boxes *and* some extra people.

The real leadership challenge comes in when you need to deal with the empty boxes and the extra people. It's really hard when you need to move someone off your team who has done well in the past, but they are no longer a fit for one of the new roles moving forward. You can't fire them for being poor performers, because they are not.

Leaders often get stuck here because this is the uncomfortable part. This is a great person—a hard worker, loyal employee, gets-things-done-kind-of-guy-or-gal—but they are just not thinking and working strategically enough. They are so busy getting old and current things done that they spend no time thinking about whether or not they should still be doing these old or current things. They are great at resolving problems, but not at transforming the situation so that the problems don't exist any more. Some people just can't let go of running the machinery to decide if they could improve or reinvent the machinery—or if different machinery entirely is what is needed.

You need someone in the role who will help you with the new thinking. Someone who will personally conceive of and lead the change, then motivate and develop the people in their own organization to move the business forward.

It's Not Personal

Here is the best way I have found to deal with this difficult situation.

You never have to "take someone out of their job." Instead, you eliminate the old role and paint a clear picture of the new role necessary to drive the new business outcome. This is why it is so important that you describe every role in your new organization as a *new* role.

Then the conversation is not, "I don't think you are capable of doing this job anymore," which feels like a personal attack or failure. Instead, the conversation becomes, "The job that you were doing does not exist any more. There is a new role in the new organization in this area that supports the new business strategy in the following ways . . ."

Then you need to explain how the new role is bigger and/or different. The easiest way to do this is to use the simple structure in Figure 9.1. The more clearly you can articulate the difference about what is expected in the new role, the easier the conversation gets. You can talk about new scope, new responsibilities, different outcomes, or the need to influence more broadly. Often the person will see the gap before you have to explain it.

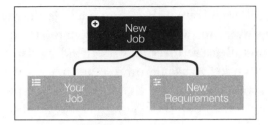

Figure 9.1   Defining the New Role

If they don't see the difference or the gap, and they believe they can do the new role, let them know that they are welcome to interview. If they don't make the cut, then you can move them sideways, down, or out. But you are not simply removing them from their role. You have eliminated a role that is no longer necessary, you have defined a new role that is necessary (which subsumes the old role and has a bunch of new stuff too), and you have given them an opportunity to interview.

SOME OF MY OWN LESSONS ABOUT REORGANIZATIONS

The reorganization I described earlier was quite dramatic. I indeed had some empty boxes and some extra people. I had to convince some people to take jobs that were far different than their expectations.

For example, I had seven general managers who rather liked being general managers. So I had to convince some of the key GMs to stay on in non-GM roles leading functions. The good news was that more often than not, the functional role running the whole integrated function across all the prior business units was bigger than their former GM role—but giving up a GM role can seem like a loss.

There were many reasons why this ultimately worked and did not blow up in my face. I handled each individual situation thoughtfully and with huge respect for the individual whose job was changing. I put a lot of personal effort into re-recruiting them and letting them know that they had an opportunity to be amazing in their new role.

But the success factor that underpinned all of this was that **the resulting organization structure made sense. It matched the mission. Everyone could understand it.**

Creating an organization that truly made sense went a long way towards calming everyone who was weary from too many re-orgs in the past. People got it. Because I started with the ideal blank sheet, instead of starting by trying to figure out how to rearrange the people who were already there, I was able to create an org structure that was truly fit for purpose.

As a leader, building the right team often requires you to eliminate some people's jobs. If you have people who are not the right fit or are not capable of doing the job that needs to be done, as a leader you need to deal with that and make a change. But I have found that every time I have needed to make such a change, the impacted person has ended up better off.

Being in the wrong role is awful. When people are struggling in the wrong roles and not doing well enough, taking them out of their roles is actually good for them. It's a relief. It gives them a new opportunity to move to a different position where they can thrive and excel. After getting over the initial shock and disappointment, they are often relieved and much happier—more like they have dodged a bullet than suffered a career setback.

The other way to look at it is that if you fail to build a team that can deliver the necessary business outcomes, you may be putting everyone at risk. By preserving the wrong team out of discomfort or guilt, you may be putting several people, including yourself, out of work later. The tougher the business challenges, the stronger the team you need, and the strategy of protecting people out of loyalty instead of performance becomes more risky.

If you have to eliminate jobs to build a stronger team, it doesn't prevent you from being kind. You can help the people you need to move out get into their next job. You are still in a position to help and provide referrals. But there is no substitute for the right team. If you don't have the right team, you need to build it.

Note: Building a Team on Strengths

When you finally start thinking about putting people in boxes, it is vitally important to think about what natural strengths the person in each box needs to have to excel at that job, and make sure you put people in those roles who genuinely have those natural strengths. I do not believe that people are all interchangeable cogs. People all have unique natural gifts and strengths. And the more you can align who a person truly is with what the role truly needs to be, the more magic you make, and the better your business will run. (See also Chapter 28: Power and Trust.)

It's very important that in each role you get people who can focus their energy on doing the work, because they don't need to waste energy compensating for the fact that they are in the wrong job. Being in a job that doesn't play to your strengths is exhausting. I've been there. I'm sure you have at least one time as well. Stack the deck in your favor and make sure you are making your team decisions based on strengths.

These are hard jobs that you need to fill. There are no easy ones. All management jobs come with big problems and risks. **But when you can align the problems and risks of a role with a person whose strengths are a good match for resolving those problems and risks, everyone and the business wins.**

Your Ideal Team Is Only the Right Team for You

It's also important to recognize that if you build the perfect team, it will only be the perfect team because you are the leader. You have a unique set of gifts and strengths (and flat spots too). So when you create your ideal org chart, it's important to make sure you include people who fill in for your flat spots. Your perfect team would not necessarily be the perfect team for a different leader who has different strengths than you.

Note: Innovation vs. Legacy

One thing that I think is worth calling out here is that I often see leaders having roles in their ideal org chart for people to take care of or optimize a legacy business, while some other roles are to innovate and build new lines of business. They fear that they will have trouble convincing someone to take on the role of managing a legacy business. They are concerned that they will lose the person because the job is not innovative (i.e., interesting or fun) enough.

It's a mistake to think that everyone wants the innovative jobs.

There are some people whose natural strengths, gifts, and interests are much more aligned with optimizing an organization than inventing a new business. It can be as demotivating (and unsuccessful) to ask an optimizer to innovate as it can be to ask an innovator to take on a "boring" optimization role. So when you think about your ideal, blank-sheet org chart, remember that there are people who truly thrive and have strengths aligned with doing one or the other.

Note: Incumbents and Strong Personalities

Another important thing to watch for when you are trying to scale is that organizations often have a tether to projects that should not move forward, solely because there is a strong incumbent or someone with a strong personality attached to the program or project. No one can imagine shutting that project down because this person has in some manner achieved an untouchable, special status in the organization.

As a leader you must assess all programs and projects from the same unemotional basis regardless of their legacies, political clout, or popularity. If they need to be stopped, tuned, or (gasp) need a different leader to take the business into the future and scale it, you must make that change. It will never happen on its own, and if it's one of the things holding you back, you need to deal with it.

Don't Forget About Redefining Your Own Box! Prepare Yourself

I also recommend going through the same process to redefine your own role. Draw the new box above your box, and realize that your new job is a combination of your current job and a box of new stuff that you are not doing yet (Figure 9.2). You need to figure out what that new stuff is and prepare yourself to step up too.

What new things does the business require that mean that *you* need to change the way that you work? Just like for all the other boxes, don't start with your name in it. Really think about what the business needs that person to do. You always need to be defining new requirements, not only for your team but also for yourself, depending on how the business is changing and evolving. If you don't know what that is, get help. Get input from others. Ask your mentors. Ask people in other companies

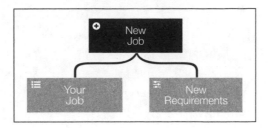

Figure 9.2   Redefining Your Role

who have similar roles. Always be challenging yourself to step up, and if you don't know exactly how, get help.

Do an Honest Assessment

You need to be brutally honest about what your desired outcome is, and what the right organization structure is to deliver it. Don't sign up for a transformation if you are unwilling to change your team or challenge yourself to grow. It's rare that you can accomplish totally new things with the exact same team that got you to where you are today. If you are unwilling to change your team, then pick a strategy that you can accomplish with the team you have. Going forth with a new, ambitious strategy, which does not match your team, will not end in success—and it will be really painful along the way for everyone.

NEXT

Once you have the structure right, you need to get the right people on board and eliminate the ones who are holding you back.
   Read on . . .

CHAPTER 10

The People

How to Attract the Right People and Eliminate the Wrong People

THE *RIGHT* PEOPLE: ALWAYS BE RECRUITING

There are some leaders that seem to have a golden touch for hiring great talent. The one thing I find in common among executives who make a lot of good hires is that they are always looking. Always.

The best way to find stars and other high caliber, talented people that you need on your team is to never stop looking for them. Don't wait for a position to open up. Keep your eyes open for them and build relationships with them. (You can't have too many top performers in your network at any level.) Then recruit them whenever you get the chance.

In corporations, open requisitions come and go, and you don't always need a new hire. To always be looking seems kind of counter-intuitive. But the reality is that you can't always find a great person when you need them and have an open spot—and you sometimes find them when you least expect it (and don't specifically need them or have an open spot).

It's not easy to do, but if you make it a habit to always be on the search for talent, when you find someone truly exceptional, it may be that you can make a spot for them. Or you could recommend them to a colleague. It's hard to change your organization structure to accommodate a random person, but I've seen many leaders get it done. What they typically do is to bring the person on in a program role, because they don't have a perfect spot for them. If the person is truly a star, they start running circles around lower performers and restructuring becomes an obvious option over time. The leader is left with a stronger team.

Be Smarter Than I Am, Please

To find and hire the best people all starts with the fundamental frame of mind that you actually want to hire the best people!

I have been continually amazed at how many managers are threatened by having really smart, capable people working for them. I have never understood this. People who have a psychological need to be the smartest person in the room and therefore avoid hiring really smart people are creating more problems for themselves than they are solving. Everyone around these people notices that they are nervous, threatened, and defensive. And if they don't ever let their team members outshine them, their organization never gets any bigger than they are. What a shame!

I can remember the first time as a manager when I had a big, scary problem to solve (and I literally had no idea how to solve or even approach it). I called a few people on my team together to discuss it. I honestly did not know what the outcome of this meeting would be, but I think I hoped that they might bring enough context to the discussion that I could find a hook to go solve it myself.

What happened was even better.

First, they started discussing the problem in front of me. I cannot stress enough that I had no value whatsoever to add to the content of solving this problem. After about 20 minutes they had articulated the problem in a way that invited an action plan, and one of them said, "I'll do this and have it done in two weeks." At this point my job was to say, "Okay. Great."

I remember this moment because it was so exciting to me to understand that my team was capable of doing things bigger and better than I could. The other related bit of delight happened the first time I delegated something that I *thought* I was good at, and then the person came back having done it far better than I would have.

These two experiences generated a big "aha" in my career.

**If you build a team where everyone is smarter
than you are, your team can accomplish
things much bigger than you can—and
that's the goal!**

Your Team Should Make You Bigger

You should not be the constraint that makes your team smaller by requiring that everything go through you, because you need to feel big and important personally. Here is one of my favorite metaphors about this: *Insisting that you remain the most important person on the team as the leader is like buying a team of thoroughbred race horses and then only ever driving them around in the trailer!*

Smart People Hire Smart People

On the contrary, when leaders hire super-smart, super-capable people and let them run and become famous as top performers, the performance of the organization goes up—and the glory always rubs off on the leader.

Let's look at the model in it's purest form: If smart people hire only even-smarter people, and those people hire only even-smarter people, the organization gets even stronger and smarter as it grows. The organization can deliver more and more. The leader is a hero.

If leaders are threatened by smart people, and hire people less smart than they are, and so on, the entire organization gets more weak and stupid over time. The leader washes out because the organization can't deliver or compete.

But let's look at this from the perspective of one manager and one really smart person. As a manager, consider if you find yourself saying, "Wow, this person is really smart, and really capable. In reality, they could do my job, maybe even better than me."

You have two basic choices in relation to your hires:

1. Uh-oh—Be threatened and lock them in a supply closet.
2. Hurray!—Pile the work on, shine a spotlight, and let them move mountains for you.

In the first case, if you are threatened and hold them back, what do you accomplish?

- You create a temporary façade of being the smartest person in the room.
- Your organization delivers less work overall.
- You piss off a high performer.
- You may "get rid of them," and that may be your goal.
- You lose the respect and support of your team because they see you don't value good people.
- Your organization delivers even less output over time.
- You are eventually seen by all as an ineffective leader.

In the second case, if you support them to thrive, what do you accomplish?

- You have another person working at your level or better, so your team delivers more.
- You can delegate virtually all your current work to someone you can trust to get it done right.
- You free up your time to think about and work on even higher value things.
- You free up time to build even more capacity into your team and broaden its impact.
- You motivate a high performer.
- You become known for attracting stars and developing talent.
- You are seen as actually being the most valuable person in the room because people see you winning the loyalty and support of a really smart, talented person.
- You personally are getting someone ready for a big promotion.
- You are building favor with someone who will likely be in a position of importance in the future.

I cannot see a single downside to letting a really smart person be as good as they can be.

I have never seen a smart person letting a smarter person thrive beneath them get damaged by this. It's good for you; it's good for them; it's good for the business. But, on the contrary, I have often seen people who are threatened by smart people so they limit them to appear more qualified personally. Those leaders lose the game. It's a shame.

Hire for Creative Problem Solving

When I talk to executives, often they lament the fact that their mid-level managers are not strategic enough. One colleague described it as follows: when there is something ambiguous and difficult to accomplish I need someone who can operate independently. I want to be able to hand them a flashlight and a PowerBar™ and say, "Go."

You need smart people who can solve problems and figure out what to do without you needing to do all the important thinking for them. It's important to look for creative problem solving skills in your interview process, so that you can find those people who you can send off to fix, solve, create, or improve things on their own.

Here is a story about creative thinking that I love that I heard many years ago. This has become a bit of urban legend and things have been added to it over time. You can find it in Wikipedia under The Barometer Question: http://en.wikipedia.org/wiki/Barometer_question.

There was a science class and there was a homework problem, which was the following:

> If you needed to find out the height of a tall building using only a barometer, how would you do it?

The "correct" answer involved measuring the air pressure at the top of the building and on the ground, and using the difference in air pressure to calculate the height of the building. Kids that used that approach and got the math right were marked correct and given full credit. But there were two other answers that stood out to me, that the teacher marked wrong with no credit. I would have marked these correct and given these two students jobs!

The First "Wrong" Answer   One student said he would take the barometer to the top of the building, drop it off, count how many seconds it takes to hit the ground, and calculate the height based on the time of the fall. This is probably at least as accurate an answer as using the air pressure-based approach.

The Second "Wrong" Answer—Even Better This student said, "I would find the general manager of the building and say to him, 'If you tell me how tall this building is, I will give you this barometer.'" Fantastic! Not only did this solution meet the requirements of solving the problem, it was likely to produce a far more accurate answer than the correct answer based on air pressure!

What a shame that these two students were marked wrong. These are precisely the kind of creative thinking skills that help people solve important problems when the by-the-book way does not work.

When you are hiring, identify creative problem solving skills by looking for interesting, nonstandard, creative solutions that people have used in the past to create success. Here are some do's and don'ts that I have learned to identify creative problem solving skills and to not get led astray by other tempting, seemingly important factors that are actually far less valuable than creative problem solving.

FIVE COMMON HIRING MISTAKES: DO'S AND DON'TS

1. Admiring a Past Accomplishment Too Much

Very often a candidate will have an accomplishment in their past that is truly extraordinary. It's more impressive than anything you've ever done personally, and far outshadows the accomplishments of the other candidates. *Wow! You're Hired!*

> **Don't:** Even though you are super excited about this accomplishment, don't hire the candidate based on this one grand accomplishment alone.

> **Don't:** Assume this breakthrough will automatically be repeated for you. Extraordinary accomplishments are very much rooted in the context of the situation. Your context and situation may not provide such an opportunity. You need to figure out what else they can do and how much of that success was theirs vs. the particular situation.

Do: Make sure they are ahead of the pack on many of the other hiring needs too.

Do: Make sure to get them to talk about how they will think, learn about, and do the specific things you need done now and in the future—don't assume brilliant success on the prior thing will automatically translate to brilliant success on what you need done.

Stories: Remember to interview them about other things! Ask for stories about how the world was different when they first got into a previous job compared to how it is now. What did they think needed to be done? What new ideas did they come up with? What changes did they drive? If they just did the job as-is for a few years, and did not grow the responsibility or usefulness of their role, they are not a creative thinker.

Actual Problems: Tell them a situation that you are facing that needs a solution. Ask them to talk through how they would approach it. Look for not only insights but also creative problem solving skills.

2. Putting Too Much Stock in Advanced Degrees

I know plenty of people with advanced degrees who are highly effective business leaders, but I know as many who are not. Advanced degrees alone are not proof of future business success. They are only proof that the person is capable of getting advanced degrees.

Don't: Say "Wow, look at all those masters and PhDs—you must be better than all the others who don't have them."

Do: Get them to talk about examples of how they have done things like you need done.

Do: Get them to give examples of how they personally conceived of and led business or organizational change.

3. Considering Only Experience, Not Advancement

I learned this lesson very early in my career when I hired a guy for a telemarketing position. I had no experience in telemarketing. I was in my twenties and he had 20 years of experience in telemarketing. I was so impressed!

I later figured out that the reason he spent twenty years in telemarketing is that he was not very good! So he never advanced.

> **Don't:** Hire someone *only* because they have a huge amount of experience in the thing you need done. Maybe they have so much experience in that job because they were never good enough at it to get promoted! If you are in need of and hiring a niche expert, you may be okay, but if you are hiring a leader, be suspicious. You are always better off judging and hiring for brainpower, motivation, and future capability than past experience—because the problems and opportunities are always changing.

When you keep your interview focused only on the spec of what is needed to be done in the job, you will attract people with very impressive experience and just the right skills to do the job that needs to be done right now. These hires are so tempting because you can see how they will immediately take some pain away. But, what about when the world changes and the job changes?

More often than not, if you've made your hire based solely on experience matching short-term needs, when the world changes around them, they get stuck. They don't adapt easily. They need to find another job that matches their skills because they are not creative and capable enough to step up to conceive of and do the new job that needs to be done. The most valuable hires are the ones who can do the job today and who also can learn and adapt quickly.

> **Do:** Look for *advancement* on a resume over experience.
>
> **Do:** Look for fast learners.

4. Falling in Love with the Personality over the Capability

Okay, when after the interview you want to go out for drinks with the person even more than you want to work with them, make sure you are not mistaking how much you like the person as a potential friend with making the right hiring decision.

> **Don't:** Make this decision alone.
>
> **Do:** Get others' help validating the person's capabilities and fit for the job.

5. Failing to Check References

This seems so obvious, but for all the reasons listed previously, I have seen people not bother, or get too busy, or need to move too fast to check references. Then they get surprised and burned. In all cases, add this to the *Do* list: Check references!

> **Don't:** Ever *not* check references.
>
> **Do:** Always check back channel references, not just the ones they give you.

How to Hire a Star

I want to talk a bit more about understanding what is in the DNA of a true star and what it takes to hire them. Stars are rare. You get to work with perhaps a handful of them throughout your career. But if you can get one in your organization, you have a big advantage while they are there.

Experience vs. Everything Else

Specific experience is rarely the primary indicator of star power. True stars are all about potential. **For stardom, you need to prioritize potential over experience.**

I have seen stars hired from totally different industries with totally different experiences than any of the other candidates. I've hired stars from odd places in the organization because I recognized the star potential and trusted them to come up to speed very quickly on the parts of the job they didn't know. When assessing if you see a star, here are some of the important clues to look for:

1. **Fast or Weird Advancement**

    If a star has been working for 10+ years, they have held progressively bigger roles. There are some big leaps and weird transitions on their resume. When you look at their resume, you're just dying to hear the story about how they went from working on a manufacturing line, to forming a band, then managing the procurement department, and then to running the global customer service organization.

    If you are interviewing a new hire out of school, there are similar advancement clues such as that they ran the events program at their college, contributed articles to *New York* magazine, built a non-profit organization from scratch, or produced a radio show—you get the point.

    Stars have a track record of advancing and doing things that were bigger than their jobs and more than their peers. Stars don't stay in the same role for years and years.

1. **Ambition**

    Stars are ambitious. They are going somewhere. They don't need you; they merely need a vehicle to get them to their next bigger or more interesting role. (This is a good thing.)

    You don't get to keep a star forever. Stars are talented and hungry. They are on the move.

    They will move mountains for you, and then they will move on. Don't be afraid of, or threatened by, rising stars. Stars are self-motivated to achieve great things for you. Enjoy it while you can and then support them to move up and onward. If you hire with the assumption that you want an experienced person who will stay in this job forever, that is what you will get. But you won't get a star.

2. **Really Smart**

    There is no substitute for raw intelligence. Sure, you need people skills, too, but stars typically have both. Stars are motivated by learning and have a track record of learning on the job (fast) and advancing beyond peers. One year of experience for a star can equate to many years of experience for someone else, because stars learn so much faster, and just go faster than everybody else.

As an example, one time a star I was mentoring told me the following: "I remember early in my career getting turned down for jobs when I didn't have experience in a particular area. The hiring manager would say something like, 'Well, you've got solid direct channel experience (based on my results and interview discussion), but you don't have any indirect channel experience, which is what we need.' I would always be amused thinking, *If only they knew that my direct channel experience—which they were so impressed by and thought was so solid—was only about three months!* I was a fast learner and doer. The things I had 'a lot' of experience in compared to the things that I had 'no' experience in were often separated by only a few months! I was grateful to sometimes find hiring managers who hired me for my potential, and not my specific experience. And I did not let them down."

Stars Are Not Easy Hires

When I've had the opportunity to hire stars, they have always had less direct experience in the job than their competition. But they had at least a few of the traits previously described.

It is tough to get them on board because stars always have other choices and multiple offers, *and* your hiring committee will think you are taking a big risk. So no one is helping you get them in the boat. The star is saying "I don't need you," and your stakeholders are saying, "We don't want her." You need to sell both parties, to get the person in the door. It is very important that you are prepared to fight for stars.

Eyebrows will rise when you choose the less "experienced" individual, but if you choose a star, they will come up to speed very quickly and everyone will quickly and ultimately be impressed and appreciative at what a good hire you have made. I've had the good fortune of doing this a handful of times in my career. It was always hard and it was always worth it. People always thought I was wrong or crazy in the beginning, and they always came around to understand just how good the person was.

Stars Are Not Easy to Find

It is not realistic to think that you can hire only stars. There are just not enough of them. Stars are rare. The few stars that do exist are hiding either because they are already working, or they don't realize that they are stars. You need to actively seek them out. Sometimes you need to let them know that they are stars and convince them that they can do more than they think.

The *Wrong* People: How to Eliminate the People Who Are Impeding Progress

This Person Is Driving Me Crazy!

There are many types of "the wrong person" issues that can manifest at any level in the organization:

Brilliant asshole: One minute they are brilliant and the next minute they are pissing everyone off. It goes back and forth forever.

Bully: This person is doing important work but is torturing peers and subordinates, and sometimes me! It's damaging to the team.

Checked out: I can't get this person to engage or take ownership for anything.

Too invested in the past: Every time we try to make progress, this person comes up with reasons why it can't be done or it's wrong to do it, citing that the legacy thing is too precious to change.

Negative: No matter what anyone says, this person speaks only of doom, and complains about everything being not good enough, stupid, slow, wrong, annoying, impossible, not competitive, the building is ugly, the technology is out of date, the donuts are from the wrong shop . . .

Saboteur: No matter what I say or do, this person is trying to secretly undermine me behind the scenes.

Not strategic: I need to keep stepping in to make all the decisions because this person is too tactical. They are good at solving problems but not good at transforming the situation to eliminate the problems.

Not performing: The work simply isn't getting done.

What Everyone Is Thinking

"Why is this person still here? He must be blackmailing someone important."

Don't ever think that your relationship with a bad performer is just between the two of you. Every minute you don't deal with it, everyone is watching and they are judging *you* as much as the poor performer.

DOES THIS PERSON NEED TO GO?

Even with the best intentions of creating the right organization structure, there still might be times when you have the wrong people on your team. It can't be avoided completely. Anyone who has been a manager has made a bad hiring choice at one time or another. Or maybe the role evolved and the person is no longer suited. Or maybe the person went through some trouble and changes in their life and they are no longer motivated, or they have become very negative.

If you are struggling with someone who is not performing and who is always causing some kind of trouble, or who is a negative drain on the morale of the team, you need to deal with it.

When someone isn't doing what you need them to do, a leader will often question themselves and say, "Is the problem truly with the person? Or might the problem be with me? Could I be a better manager? Should I be doing something different when I am delegating, communicating, or supporting the person? It doesn't seem fair to fire the person if the fault is really mine and I just have not figured out how to be a good enough manager for them."

Can't or Won't

The simple decision tree in Figure 10.1 has helped me quickly get out of this quandary.

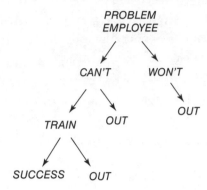

Figure 10.1   Can't or Won't

Is the reason the person is not performing because they "can't" (meaning they are not capable or trained), or because they "won't" (meaning they don't want to)? So, what should you do when you are not sure if it's a can't or a won't? (Though you are pretty sure it's a "not"!)

Find Out

You need to have a conversation. Start the conversation in a frank but constructive way. Start with trust and good intentions.

"Your performance has not met the expectations we agreed upon. What do you think the problem is?"

Sometimes this one question is all you need to ask. If they don't want to do the work for some reason, it will often come out. "I don't agree with this, I don't support this, etc."

But if their answer is not clear, you can simply ask, "Do you have an issue with what is being asked of you? Do you believe this task is necessary and important? Is your intention to deliver on this at or above expectations?"

Intentions Are Important

If they let you know that they disagree or don't support what you are trying to do, give them a choice to make. Will you support the plan or not? If they say no, then they are a "won't" and you follow the "out" path.

If they say yes, then find out how motivated they are to improve. If they convince you that they are on board and they truly want to do the work, then they are a "can't." Ask them what they are struggling with. Ask them what they need to do a better job. If someone is genuinely motivated, they will take personal ownership for the performance issue and their development, and will ask for help. Then you can give an honest try of training and support.

If they say they support the plan but then don't take personal responsibility for the performance gap, and they resist help, or blame you or others, or complain that their chair is the wrong color, these are all additional versions of "won't." Then you follow the "out" path.

Benefits of Removing "Won'ts" from Your Team

I can't count how many times an executive has brought me in with the goal to help get his team functioning and executing better—but after a bit of time I realized that how the team was working together was not the problem. The problem was one person. There was one person blocking progress, sabotaging communication, dragging morale down—a won't.

Poor performance is contagious. The overall performance of your team is defined more by the lowest performer than the highest. Negativity has a way of spreading, so it's important to rid your organization of negativity.

My experience has been, 100 percent of the time, that getting a won't out has a remarkably positive impact:

- *You* will be more productive, as you will no longer waste time dealing with the variety of annoying, draining, damaging, needing to be corrected or reworked, not good enough, or otherwise apologized-for issues that this person causes.
- Everyone feels the positive impact that results from the negative energy being removed. The motivation and productivity of the whole team goes up, *even if they have to cover the work.*
- Your top performers stay motivated to keep performing when they see that you address poor performance, and show that good performance counts for something.

Removing low performers, though it is a draining and unpleasant activity in the short term, has a big impact on the success of your business in the long term, not to mention on your own career and your sanity.

Bullies

I feel compelled to make a special note about bullies. Unfortunately, the workplace is scattered liberally with them—people who have a need to make others feel bad by being abusive or dismissive. Remove bullies from your organization. It can be tempting to keep a bully in their role because they are often very talented and productive. Sometimes they are even charming and persuasive. Bullies can go fast because they don't feel the slightest hesitation to leave casualties in their path.

If your bullies are so brilliant and productive and you truly can't live without them, isolate them, don't let them be managers, and protect the rest of the organization from them. If you make the choice to keep a bully, make it with your eyes open, and make sure you are doing something to protect the people they work with. If you plan to support a bully in your ranks, I believe that you have a moral obligation to help the other people in your organization not get injured. Don't leave this to sort itself out. It won't, and it will cause a lot of damage in the mean time.

Everyone Is in the Biggest Job They've Ever Had

When I get called in by a business who is having trouble scaling their business, one of the things I always ask is, "When you look around the table at your staff, how many of your people are in the biggest job they've ever had?" If the answer is "everyone," it is a red flag.

Some people will be able to scale. But if everyone on the team is in the biggest job they've ever had, you need to recognize that no one in the room even knows what the goal looks like! If no one has ever seen how things are done at the size of company you aspire to, it's a big risk. If you want to double or quadruple your business, you need to have some leaders on your team who have worked at that scale. Because if you want to scale, you need to start building things as they will operate when you are bigger—before you get there. And if no one on your team has ever even seen what that looks like, let alone done it, it is very difficult to get there.

> **You need some people who not only know what the future looks like, but who have done their roles in much bigger companies.**

Recruiting people with experience at a bigger scale is actually pretty easy to do. They may have been a director-level manager in an $800M supply chain operation, and you are giving them the opportunity to be an EVP of supply chain for a $200M business. So although the numbers are smaller, they personally get to run the whole show and build something. I have hired several people who have been motivated by exactly this.

Note to the leader: If you are the one who is in the biggest job you've ever had, I'm not suggesting you need to resign! But you need to do three things:

1. Get a mentor who is not in your chain of command who can point out your blind spots, teach you what you need to do to scale, and help you network with peers at bigger companies.
2. Hire some people who have been in bigger jobs and trust them.
3. Be open to not doing everything the way you have always done it.

THE RIGHT TEAM WILL GET YOU THERE

Expect that leading change and getting an organization to stick to it through the long Middle will be exhausting—because it is. Transformation always feels like extra work on top of too much current work. So don't shoot yourself in the foot by tolerating a weak or negative person or a legacy role that is fighting against you. If you can get even just one or two truly remarkable people on your team, your chance of success (not to mention your own health and sanity) over the long term will rise exponentially.

NEXT

Building a great team in any moment is only part of your job. The other part of your job is to make sure that your team is always getting more capable. Read on . . .

CHAPTER 11

Building Capacity

Performance Management and Delegating for Development

WHAT EVERYBODY IS THINKING

If I do an excellent job and deliver against my objectives, I'm a top performer.

The vast majority of people in corporations think that high performance = doing their job well. Many do not realize that high performance is found outside the boundaries of one's job description. A job description is valid only for a moment in time. Then the world changes. High performers realize that they have to break through the limits of their job description and do things over and above it to meet evolving business needs and to develop themselves.

But for the majority of people, if no one has ever given them coaching or the idea that it is important to build their own capability, their tendency will be to keep doing the same work as it was defined for them in the beginning.

Why this happens is so interesting to me, and it has to do largely with a shift that must occur in our self-awareness after finishing school and starting work. Here is what I am referring to. In school, an advancing curriculum is given to you every year. You start school as a small child and learn how to count and sing and finger paint, and then if you master those tasks, you move on to the next year, and you learn how to read and write and do math. Each year after completing the work given to you, you advance to the next grade, where you're given a harder, more challenging set of things to learn.

Your teacher and the school provide a progressively more difficult curriculum for you. If you just show up and do what is asked of you, you will develop—and you will advance. This goes on through middle school and high school and university. But then you graduate. And then comes the dramatic change: Once you leave school . . . *no one will ever do this for you again.*

So all of us need to look beyond our job descriptions and make sure to keep advancing and developing ourselves. We need to give ourselves a progressively harder curriculum each year if we want to excel. In particular, your transformation will require that you get enough of the people in your organization motivated and actively looking outside their job descriptions to evolve their work to make your strategy come true, because **by definition, whatever the new strategic work is, it is not in people's original job descriptions.**

Always Be Growing

Leaders need to apply this development thinking to team performance as well. Your team should be getting more capable over time. Think about it this way. As the leader of a team, on day one, your team has a certain capacity. Your team can deliver a certain amount of work in a certain amount of time, at a particular level of quality and complexity. They have a certain amount of knowledge and particular level of ability to perform. This is their capacity on day one.

If, after a year goes by, you have delivered everything you have been asked, you have done part of your job. But if your team is not more capable in some way—if they can't deliver more, better, faster, or higher quality—or if they have no new knowledge, skills, or ability to perform at a higher level, you have not done the second part of your job. You have not increased the capacity of your team.

Performance Management

A critical factor in both building capability and ensuring your transformation keeps moving forward is how you do performance management. Many times we associate the term "performance management" with managing or eliminating poor performers. But there is a positive side of performance management too.

Effective performance management is as important to stimulate the development and positive performance of your team and the individuals, as it is to deal with poor performers.

Who's with Me? Connecting Performance with Transformation

In leading any kind of transformation, it's important to know who is helping you, who may be against you, and who is basically just ignoring you.

Transformation is hard. You need help. You need people who will stay in it with you through the long Middle and pull their share, and sometimes more than their share, of the weight. The average person is probably avoiding jumping in with both feet.

Performance management is not just about writing a review once a year and sitting down to an awkward conversation. Performance management can and should be about tuning performance so that your organization is clear about what behaviors are expected and rewarded and which ones are not tolerated. In a transformation it's necessary to spell it out: *[This] is the increased performance necessary and expected in your role to help drive our transformation.*

Willingness, ability, and motivation to personally lead transformation needs to be something that you measure people on, and give them stretch goals for.

You need to build the behaviors you want to see in supporting your transformation into people's performance objectives at all levels of the organization. In a transformation, you want to inspire your top performers to really stretch and you want to make it clear to the people who are not actively helping that they are not meeting expectations.

In a transformation it's too easy for people to hide. Without rigorous performance management, your strategy is at risk.

Lack of clarity about performance expectations related to the transformation creates opportunities every day to ignore the important new work that needs to get done during the Middle.

A good way to start the transformation-performance conversation is to ask each of your team members to suggest performance measures for themselves that relate to the transformation. You will be able to tell right away how bought in they are and if they are willing and able to conceive of and lead the change you need, based on their inputs.

Whatever your company's official performance management process might be, from formal and rigid to sloppy or nonexistent, you have an opportunity to overlay something useful to support your transformation from whatever the existing process is.

THE GOAL: NO SURPRISES

In my work I talk to lots of people in lots of organizations. And most of them are not getting feedback. It's a shame. I see more leaders who avoid doing performance management than ones who do it well. It is very common that the leader thinks that they have communicated clearly to their direct report, but when he or she talks to the direct report, they have no clue what their manager is thinking.

What Everyone Is Thinking:

How am I doing? Does anybody see me? Is my work valued? Does the company appreciate my hard work? I don't really get much feedback. My manager never talks to me about my performance. When can I get a promotion? How can I get a raise?

Nothing about a person's performance should come as a surprise—ever. To you or to them. Here is an example of what I mean by a surprise. If the employee thinks they are doing a good job, and that they have support and are well regarded, but at the same time, the leader believes there is a performance problem, there is going to be a surprise. If they don't talk about it, by the time a performance review, a ranking, a bonus cycle, or worst case, a layoff happens, that employee is in for a terrible surprise. It's not fair to the employee, and it's not good for the business.

As a leader, if you set your goal as "no surprises" for the quality of performance management you are doing, and if you achieve the goal that no one on your team is ever surprised, that will create all kinds of good outcomes. "No surprises" is actually a good example of a control point as discussed in Chapter 4: Control Points. To achieve that one outcome, you will have to do a bunch of things right: set clear goals, discuss them, communicate expectations and impressions, and agree on measures and follow up on them.

If you never have performance conversations, you miss the opportunity to inspire better performance!

As a leader, you should be communicating expectations and sharing yours and others' views of the performance of an employee at least twice a year. As an employee, if you are not getting this from your manager, you should drive the process. You need to ask, "How am I doing?" How am I doing compared to your expectations? Compared to others? Do you see me as meeting, achieving, or overachieving on my goals? Here is what I think—are we on the same page?"

My view on this is if you are either the manager or the employee, prioritize the performance conversation.

Because I have always believed that the performance conversation is so important, in my own career for 17 years I drove the discussion about my performance with my boss when he was not doing it.

Regular Review

There is no downside to having clear, regular performance conversations, and in fact this is one of the most important traits of being a good manager. You should also be setting expectations for and measuring your managers on doing no-surprise performance management with their teams.

Clarity is your friend here. Strive to be super clear, not only with regard to timelines and deliverables, but also with regard to expectations about communication, leadership, judgment, influence, innovation, growing a team, and (don't forget) supporting the transformation. A performance conversation should also be developmental. There should be a conversation about stretch goals and building on strengths.

Building capability in general should be part of every performance conversation.

If you are very clear about expectations and measures in the first performance conversation, in the next one, you can simply refer to the data: "Here's what we talked about last time." If there are gaps, you can address them simply by saying, "Let's talk about this gap. We agreed to this. What happened? What do you think? What have you learned? What do you propose?" The conversation never needs to get awkward or emotional if you have been clear and you have the data from past conversations.

DELEGATING = DEVELOPING

If you want to build the capability of your team, a good place to start is with your top performers. If you can get your top performers to step up, you can free yourself up to do bigger and better things. Think how much more you and your team could do if you had some people on your team as capable as you are. Think of the important, strategic work you could do if you could delegate more big stuff to top performers. Think about how much more energy you could put into leading your transformation if you could clear your plate of much of the work you have now.

Develop High Performers Like Successors

I learned the lesson of what truly effective delegating is when I started to think about and do succession planning. The big "aha" for me was that if I needed to develop a successor, that was serious development for someone. And then I thought, *why not do this type of development even if succession is not the goal?*

> **One of the biggest tools you have for development is delegating. It's important to think about delegating not just as assigning work, but as a technique for teaching, developing, and building capacity in your organization.**

The only true way to develop a successor is to delegate a lot of your job so that someone else can practice doing it. By delegating bigger and bigger stuff to someone as though you were developing someone as a successor, you are actually maximizing that person's development. Think about getting a couple of your top performers ready to step into your job. What could be more impactful to increasing the capacity of your team? This is relevant at every level of management.

Here are three important ways to use the succession idea as you delegate for maximum development. And if your goal is in fact to develop a successor, these are still the right things to do:

1. **Let them practice your work**

    The first part of someone learning your job is about the work. You need to give them opportunities to practice working at your level.

    A lot of times we think the way to motivate our top performers is to have them work on the most fun or interesting projects. That works to a point, but it does not do anything to help get someone ready for your job. Face it, how much fun work do *you* get to do?

    You need to give them opportunities to practice the ugly, mind-numbing, heavily matrixed, controversial, boring, unsupported, no-win kind of work you deal with every day when you wake up. What is the hardest and most distasteful thing you own? That's what you give your top performer! You give them the benefit of seeing what it is really like to be in your shoes. They get to suffer like you do. But they get to work on big stuff. They get access to your network and stakeholders. They have the chance to do something creative and heroic to get this done.

Don't shy away from giving smart people hard work.

2. Let them practice your relationships

The next part of getting someone ready for your job is to make sure they are practiced and comfortable with the social requirements at the next level. They need to be someone that your peers feel comfortable with and want to include personally. They can't stand out like a sore thumb as the junior person in the room, who has no basis for being there.

You need to give your top performer a chance to practice these relationships. Give them opportunities to present for you. Arrange one-on-one meetings with them and your peers. Send them as your delegate to your boss's staff meeting when you are out of town. (Go out of town if this never happens.) If your top performer does not develop personal relationships with your boss and peers, they will not be capable of stepping in for you to free you up—because they will not be given the chance.

3. Let them practice your decisions

Okay. Here is where the rubber meets the road. You need to give someone a chance to practice making the decisions that you make. **If you never delegate important decisions, you are fooling yourself that you are truly developing someone.**

Think about the next few months of decisions you need to make: investments, priorities, partnerships, product road map choices, marketing strategies. Give your top performer the task of owning the project *and* making the decisions. Let them feel the pressure of owning the outcome fully. Let them get the experience explaining, defending, and selling their choices. Let them get the experience fixing it if it goes wrong.

Is this scary? Yes. Might they choose wrong? Yes. Might they choose better than you? Also yes. The point is, if you never let them own and make key decisions, you are cutting off the single most important training you can give your successor. They will never be ready for your job without owning key decisions.

FAILURE IS THE KEY TO DELEGATING

Delegating some of your decisions opens up the risk of people getting it wrong. This can be scary but it is one of the most powerful ways that we all learn. There is no learning as great as that which comes after failing. Many managers treat delegating exactly the opposite, as if it is their role to prevent failure by watching closely, jumping in and taking over, and fixing or modifying if it is not going well. If you think about this from a learning perspective, what you have just done is to ensure that no real learning occurs. By always averting failure personally, you inadvertently take away the person's motivation, need, and ability to learn.

It's kind of like teaching a child to ride a bike, by holding on and running alongside—and then never letting go—ever. For the rest of your life, you'll be running alongside, holding on to prevent the potential fall.

Think how much farther they could ride, and how many new things they could discover, if you weren't still hanging on, running alongside and slowing them down.

So what happens if someone fails?

Well, when you fail it feels bad. It is embarrassing. It causes business problems, It causes trouble for other people—so it becomes a big personal motivator to fix it! Real learning occurs when you not only see what you did wrong, but need to live with and deal with the consequences of what you did wrong.

By creating the safety net and filling in all the hard parts for them, the person never really learns and never gets to truly experience what it means to succeed. But if you let a smart person fail, they will figure it out. Isn't that how you got good at what you do? By doing it—trial and error, feedback, trying again. A smart person will learn how to really do it well if you give them a chance.

Also, if you always swoop in to save the day, you are ensuring that they will never get any better at the task than you are.

You are putting an artificial cap on their development. Why not give them the chance to get even better at it than you are? I have often delegated things that I thought I was pretty good at, and had my employee blow me away with their ability to exceed my capabilities. This, to me, is one of the best parts of management—when you can say, "Wow, that's amazing. You did that better than I ever imagined it could be done. Bravo. Thank you. Look at this new capability my team now has!"

Fail Small or Fail Big

Admittedly this is a bit of a paradox—how do you succeed if your people are failing? Think ahead to the desired outcome. Today your team can't do the work as well as you can, so you have two choices. Do it yourself and prevent your team from growing, or take some risk in the short term, and in a year from now have a team that can do more than you ever imagined.

Pick Your Battles

Don't pick the most business critical deliverable and put it with the most junior person. But do pick a meaty task and let a smart person who can learn something run with it. Always be on the lookout for opportunities to let people own outcomes and decisions so they can truly learn in the process. Not everything important is mission critical. It is your job to manage all the outcomes so that you create the space and opportunity for people to fail, learn, succeed, and grow, while at the same time managing the overall outcome to create success.

EVERYBODY UP!

You need to create an environment where doing a bigger job to improve yourself and your team is not only allowed, it is expected. If you want the strongest team possible helping you to drive change, make sure you have people who have the insight and capability to evolve their roles, and challenge and support them to step up. Let some of them work at your level. Let them really learn. And always make sure to keep the conversations about expectations and performance clear and fluent with everyone.

NEXT

Make sure you don't hinder performance and motivation by keeping your communications at such a formal and official level that you never learn what people really think.
Read on . . .

CHAPTER 12

Unstructured Conversation

How to Drive Personal Accountability and Belief

In my work as a business advisor helping organizations execute, part of my process is to talk to everybody—well, if not actually *everybody*, I make sure to talk to many people at multiple levels in the organization. So I've talked to a lot of people at a lot of levels in a lot of organizations in a lot of industries.

What I have noticed is that many transformation efforts seem to hover at the top. They primarily include discussions of strategy with executives. But I have found that this high-level-only approach misses the most important part of a transformation.

Although you can lead a transformation from the top, you can't execute a transformation from the top.

And you can't even start a transformation if you fail to engage people at all levels in the beginning—because they hold the keys. And if *they* are not going forward, *you* are not going forward.

I, of course, talk to the executives leading the change, but in addition I talk to the leaders on their teams and others throughout the organization. I can't count how many times, though, while I am having confidential conversations with each of them, I am left thinking, "Do you people ever talk to each other?"

The executives and the people inside their organizations are often in violent agreement about how they feel, about what needs to be done, and about what role each of them should play in doing it. They are completely frustrated with the other party for not understanding. An executive will tell me, "This leader just isn't getting it; I need him to show that he is changing his organization to be more innovative." And that same leader will tell me, "I'm so frustrated because I want to change my organization to be more innovative, but my boss is preventing me from making changes." (I have had this exact conversation.)

Please just talk to each other.

The Value of Unstructured Conversation

The most valuable and necessary leadership moments are not found in a spreadsheet or in a formal business review. **The most valuable moments in leadership come from the informal conversations where people let their guard down and say what they really think.**

Unstructured conversation has an enormous ability to unlock higher productivity, not to mention to greatly reduce execution risk. But you need to be willing to do it. And I notice that many executives are not.

"Make It So"

Executives seem to want to say, "Here's the situation, I need you to do this." Their expectation is that the manager will say, "Okay, will do," and come back with a programmatic response about getting it done.

While that sounds very efficient and kind of okay, it avoids any real conversation about what you are trying to get done. And many executives seem to prefer it that way. I have tried to understand why leaders avoid unstructured conversations with the people on their teams. They often dismiss it as a waste of time. Or some leaders think that they are above this type of communication. But what I believe is really going on is that they feel like unstructured conversation will be uncomfortable. I haven't really figured out all the reasons for the avoidance, but I can tell you for sure that **it's the avoiding of real conversations that invites risk in the business. And it leads to new grand strategies getting left on the shelf instead of getting implemented.**

REAL ENGAGEMENT IS ALWAYS PERSONAL

The reason unstructured conversation is uncomfortable is because instead of the safe, sterile "I want a plan . . . here is my plan" type of communication, you open yourself to a more personal conversation that might get messy. If you ask people to tell you what they really think or feel about the strategy, they might tell you what they really think or feel! And it might not be in perfect alignment. Think really seriously about this.

> **If you avoid the conversation because you don't want to hear something out of alignment, your only other choice is to go forward with that same risk, but not know about it!**

When you engage someone on a personal level and ask what they really think, you might get something personal, creative, and maybe emotional. But that's the point. **Don't you want to engage people on a creative, personal, and emotional level?**

When these unstructured conversations are not happening, performance always suffers.

Motivation also suffers—*but performance actually suffers*. Teams get stuck because the underlying belief system of the team, which needs to support whatever the organization is trying to do, is not in alignment—because you've never actually talked about it!

"What Do You Really Think?"

When I had my first major executive role with people very much my senior reporting to me, I was always scared that they would not feel okay about it.

After a short time, I realized that not only were they not uncomfortable reporting to me, they were quite happy about it. I kept on doubting and second-guessing myself, thinking, *How can it be that these very experienced people enjoy reporting to (younger, less experienced) me?* What I now realize is that a huge part of the answer is that I would regularly ask them in a sincere and unstructured way, "What do you really think?"—and that no one else had ever asked them before!

Know for Sure That You Are All Aligned

As a leader, you really need to have a high level of confidence that you and your team have aligned your belief systems about what is necessary to succeed and what you are trying to do. Otherwise there is too much risk. When you are depending on a team to execute, how could you not want to know what people really think? Are you all aligned on:

1. Why are we doing this?
2. Do we really agree about what is most important?
3. Do we share a belief system that supports the success of this mission? (For example: A growing market exists, a competitor will stumble, and a supplier will remain available.)

If you as the leader are only broadcasting what needs to be done, and your team is saying "okay," you are assuming that you all agree on the answers to these fundamental questions, but you won't know for sure unless you talk about them in a sincere and open way.

Start the Conversation Before the Official Planning and Budgets

It can be as simple as this: "Here's what I'm thinking and why? What do you really think?" **You need to invest some time to allow your team to build their own belief in whatever you want them to do.**

Belief and alignment cannot be achieved in an instant without talking about it. Each person needs time to process the ideas and form their own point of view.

> **People need unstructured conversation in order to establish their own way of believing in the strategy. They need to get their own opinions, thoughts, and beliefs in line before they will be ready to move.**

Sure, it might get messy. But you need to allow that and work through it. Your only other choice is to have people starting down the course of implementing the strategy with a lot of personal doubts and misunderstandings. When you allow the time to work though these questions, misalignments, varied expectations, and disagreements, it might feel like you are veering off course, but in reality, the opposite is true—you are enabling the team to converge on a course.

What you might not be able to see is that when you announce your new strategy, you have already created a train wreck! Everyone needs to make their own journey to the path you need them to be on. You can't simply place them on that path. The unstructured conversation is what allows everyone to find their own way to the path. You can't force it. And if you skip this step, people won't be able to execute on the new thing because their belief systems are stuck somewhere else.

> **By avoiding potentially messy conversations up front, what you have actually done is traded a false sense of order and harmony in the short term for a slow moving catastrophe where people are not effectively set up to succeed in the long term.**

I can tell you from the many leadership teams that I work with: When we allow these types of conversations to happen, and *then* build a specific plan to put the new strategy into action, it has a much higher success rate. An example of this happened very recently to me where a leader brought me in to work with his team to put an execution plan in place for a key strategic initiative in the business. But when we started the meeting, most of his peers rebelled. Instead of helping to work on the execution plan, they were saying things like, "I don't agree with this premise. We are not thinking broadly enough. I don't think this is the right strategy."

Oops!

So here's what I did. Instead of trying to go forward building the execution plan, I asked them all, "What do you really think?" The owner of the strategy was getting a little nervous, but I knew that we could not move forward without this step. We spent 90 minutes doing a blue ocean, blue sky conversation about big ideas and what the alternative strategy should be, and then I posed the following question to the group: "Do you believe that more study on a broader strategy will prove that this current strategy is unsound and that you shouldn't do it? Could you do something so big soon enough? Or would it be better to get this part done now?" Everyone ended up agreeing that the current proposed strategy was the right thing to do in the immediate term, and they should explore other bigger picture strategies for next steps as a parallel effort.

Then we got down to business and spent the rest of the day creating execution plans and timelines for the strategy as the leader intended.

But if we had not allowed that unstructured conversation to let everyone express their thoughts and concerns up front, we would have stalled. If we had insisted on having only the highly structured conversation about putting the proposed strategy into action, it would have been a disaster during the meeting and after the meeting. All that pent-up energy and belief about the need to do something different would have remained pent up. And instead of the team being able to align and focus on moving forward, people would have been shooting arrows at the execution plan the whole day and probably forever after.

Without unstructured conversation you risk the team's not truly engaging on a personal level, and you also risk ongoing misunderstandings, disagreements, and sabotage. *Unstructured conversation reduces risk and increases performance.*

Let people be people. Acknowledge them. Let them think. Let them speak. Unstructured conversation is a gold mine of productivity. Please don't avoid it. Strive to get genuine alignment and engagement at a personal level by giving people some time to get their own beliefs in line with what you need them to do.

NEXT

A particular form of avoiding useful conversations is status meetings. Stop having status meetings! Learn the much better things to do with your team time that will give you genuine insights to improve your business execution. Read on . . .

CHAPTER 13

Stop Having Status Meetings

Go Faster and Reduce Risk

WHAT EVERYBODY IS THINKING

I'm bored!

Status meetings are boring. They waste time. They do not move the business forward.

I think the epidemic of status meetings takes root when new managers have a staff meeting (because they know they are supposed to have staff meetings), but they are not sure what to do in their staff meeting, so they ask each person to give a status update about their work. What ensues is basically a series of one-on-one meetings between the manger and each team member while everyone else is watching (or doing email).

Then this type of behavior can also move into bigger forums, which turn into things like phase review meetings and quarterly business reviews. These meetings have lots more people from multiple teams in a room for hours or days on end to review the status of multiple projects at a level of detail that makes you want to kill yourself. To picture this meeting, imagine 30 people sitting in a room and not paying attention to the one person who is standing in the front of the room talking about slides that are densely populated with detail.

Almost everyone is looking at their laptops.

Then for each presenter there is someone in the audience who tries to sound like they are interested and accountable, who asks a couple of pointed questions to appear to be uncovering a deep insight or exposing a risk.

If you truly want to keep your strategy moving forward, stop having status meetings. Status meetings are a waste of time. Have better meetings.

STATUS MEETINGS CAUSE MORE PROBLEMS THAN THEY SOLVE

Status meetings are almost a form of anti-communication. They do not foster a healthy sharing of knowledge, ideas, and risks. They choke the system with so much detail that the insights can never appear. There are three key problems that status/review meetings cause:

1. You don't gain necessary insights about risks and opportunities.
2. You keep people from doing real work and waste a lot of time.
3. You fail to discuss the things that would give you insights about risks and opportunities because you spend all your time and energy reviewing project detail. See also Chapter 19: Detail.

What to Do Instead of Status Meetings

There are two things that you need to rework once you decide to stop having status meetings:

1. You need an alternate, effective plan to track status.
2. You need to decide what else to do at your staff meeting if you are not reviewing status.

AN ALTERNATIVE WAY TO TRACK STATUS

Find the Control Points

As we talked about in Chapter 4: Control Points, the first step in improving your ability and effectiveness in tracking progress is to define the right control points. If you are measuring the right control points, you get very solid information about the performance of your business without wading through hours of status detail.

Create a Useful Tracking Framework and Process

Once you know what the key outcomes or control points are, and have them staged out on a timeline throughout the Middle, then you can create a process and framework for each project team to report ahead of time on those key measures.

Each product team will still create and use their detailed project plans to do and manage their work, but what gets reported upwards will be a new communication-based, outcome-oriented report. This report will contain insights about the key control points for each project and how you are performing on those.

Have a Different and Better Meeting

Then when you have the staff meeting or review meeting, reading of the new reports about the control points is pre-work. It gives you a chance to flag the issues, risks, and opportunities. Those become the things you talk about in the meeting. In one company I worked for I got the quarterly business review process down from five full days per quarter to two by doing this. And the quality of the insights and output was better. Everyone was happier.

BETTER THINGS TO DO IN YOUR STAFF MEETINGS

Now that you have freed up all that status review time, here are some examples of more productive things you can be doing with staff meeting time. Start thinking about using your team when they are together to pursue higher value outcomes as a team. This is also necessary for building the capacity of your team as we talked about in Chapter 11: Building Capacity.

1. **What are the key outcomes we are on the hook for?**
   What control points should we measure? How will we know if we are achieving them?

   It's really worth putting the question of key outcomes and control points out there for team discussion, and aligning on both the control points and what the measures are. You will be surprised by how many different potential opinions exist if you

haven't had this discussion already. Going forward with dif-
fering opinions on what is important and how you measure it
results in low productivity.

2. **What are the risks we face?**

    What should we do about them?

    It's always important to remember that everyone has a
    different risk profile. You will find that some people are afraid
    of everything and others are afraid of nothing. When you talk
    about risks with your team, you'll get critical insights on how
    aligned your team's belief system is about what you are trying
    to do and how you need to manage the individuals on your
    team—and you may even learn about an important risk that
    you didn't see before.

3. **What is the data we wish we knew about our business?**

    Is it knowable? How will we find it? If it is not knowable,
    what scenarios should we plan for?

    I can tell you I made this mistake every which way for
    years . . . wishing I had data that actually was knowable, or
    guessing at answers that were not knowable. Make the list with
    your team. Get the data you can get and make explicit scenario-
    based plans for what you will all agree to do when there is no
    data.

4. **What stupid stuff are we doing?**

    I would have this as a staff topic at least twice a year. This
    one never ceases to pay off. Annoying, time-wasting stuff
    always creeps into the environment, and then teams just accept
    that as the new reality. Once or twice a year, talking about
    "what stupid stuff are we doing?" gives people the permission
    to not have to just accept the annoying, inefficient, ineffective
    stuff, but to highlight the issues causing them. Then as a team
    you can choose one or two and fix them. Productivity always
    improves after this meeting.

5. **Question the habits**

    Habit is a very powerful force that makes organizations
    get stuck doing things the same way over and over again. Old
    habits become ingrained, and some lose their usefulness. And
    then everyone gets too busy to think about how there might

be a better way to do something. One of the most useful things I repeatedly did in my career was to step outside of the current business's habits—and to really observe, question, and then improve them. I learned to always ask and investigate:

- Why do we do this?
- Who uses this? And what do they use it for?
- Have we asked them if it is useful?
- Would something else be better?
- How much does this cost and why? What do we get?

I was in a turnaround situation once where the new head of manufacturing reduced expenses by almost 30 percent by simply asking vendors, "What do we get for this cost? Why can't it be less?" The old business had gotten out of the habit of questioning the vendors, and so the vendors just kept charging and charging. Once he asked, they reduced the price!

6. **What has changed?**

What has changed in our market and business, or our customers' markets and businesses? What does that mean for our plans?

Here again, you will find that some people care deeply and know a lot, and others are happy to just keep their head down plowing away at their former job descriptions. Find out. Discuss. Drive important change.

7. **What improvements can we make?**

What process or infrastructure improvement would have the biggest impact on our ability to deliver? As the manager you are responsible for making improvements and increasing the capacity and capability of your team over time. But you don't have to think of all the answers yourself. Crowdsource it with your team. This question is actually important to ask everyone in the organization, not just your direct reports.

8. **What has become harder and easier in our work and business?**

What should we consider changing?

At the pace technology and communication changes, something is now harder or easier in your business than it was before. If competition or margins have become harder, shine the spotlight on it and discuss it as a team. If technology advances could make things easier, don't miss it. Don't keep doing things the same old, slow, hard way because you never paused to think and talk about it.

9. **What should we all be learning?**

What should we learn this year in addition to our core work? What do we want to be better at, or smarter about, next year?

Elevate the discussion about what we should all be doing (in addition to our day jobs) to improve. Make it clear that doing the job is only part of the job. Everyone should have goals to improve, and your team should be focused on "something we all need to learn or get better at" at any given point in time.

10. **Who should we thank?**

Who in our organization has done something remarkable that we should recognize?

I find that if you don't have this discussion at your regular staff meeting, all kinds of great things happen in your organization and they go unseen and therefore un-thanked. Not recognizing exceptional efforts destroys trust. Talk about this so you don't miss it! We'll talk about this more in Chapter 28: Power and Trust.

11. **Who are the stars?**

Who are the high potential people in our organization that we should be investing in developing?

Always have a short list of high potential people who should be getting extra exposure, bigger challenges, and introductions to mentors. One of the best things you can do as a leader is to grow top performers in your organization. It's good for them, for you, and for the company, and ultimately for the world!

12. **What is our team brand?**

Who/what groups should our team be communicating, networking, or improving our brand with? How should we do it?

This is a topic that always brings a lot of energy when I work with clients on leadership team building. Who are the groups that your team serves? How do they perceive you? How do you need them to perceive you? Do you have any enemies? Do you have any organizations trying to fight against what you are trying to do? Do any groups currently have a wrong assumption about your team or what it does? What is your team brand? What do you want it to be? See also Chapter 7: Sponsors and Enemies. It's useful to bring your whole team into this discussion.

Laughter

I read once that people are more productive after they have been laughing. It was not hard research but I gave it a try. I started opening my staff meetings with casual conversation, telling or inviting jokes, and getting people laughing. In the beginning everyone was concerned that I was wasting time, but I was amazed at how quickly we could get down to business and start working on hard problems together after the fun. Once I told them that I was doing this on purpose, everyone recognized how well it worked and appreciated being allowed to be less robot-like.

NEXT

Today very few of us have the luxury of working in the same building with our teams. It's important to have a strategy to build a strong and motivated team and maximize their productivity even when they are spread out all over the world. Read on . . .

CHAPTER 14

Virtual and Remote Teams

Optimizing Performance and Results from Afar

WHAT EVERYONE IS THINKING

Where is everybody? Can anybody see me?

It's very rare today that teams get to work together in the same building. And this causes worry for everyone involved. Managers are worried about productivity. Remote individuals are worried about how to build their reputations and credibility from afar. Everyone is worried about having enough influence, or being marginalized if they are not present at headquarters. People become slaves to their messaging platforms because they are afraid that someone will notice if they are not responsive for 10 seconds. Time zones and native language differences make regular, high-quality communication awkward and difficult.

There are three important ideas I would like to address for creating success (and reducing stress) with virtual and remote teams:

1. Optimizing your work-from-home policies
2. Managing and motivating a geographically dispersed team
3. Advising the remote individual

OPTIMIZING YOUR WORK-FROM-HOME POLICY

Many companies provide work-from-home options. Employees love it. But many managers struggle with it. They ask me about this all the time:

"Should we allow it? Is it a good thing for business? Is it a bad thing for business? How do you optimize motivation *and* productivity?"

To me, there is a very simple way of looking at this that removes a lot of the questions and angst about this:

Individuals can be more productive working at home, but teams can't.

It's as simple as that. Teams are always *less* productive when people are not together. Always. So your goal for your work-at-home policies should be to create a way of working that optimizes individual productivity by letting people work at home sometimes, and optimizes team productivity by having people together in the office sometimes.

Also, I have observed that if there is ever a productivity issue with people working from home, it's because expectations and measures are unclear—not because the people at home are slacking off. As we talked about in Chapter 11 with regard to performance management, clarity is your friend. If you have clear expectations, outcomes, and measures defined, it should not matter where the person works. If you don't have clear measures defined, the person can perform equally poorly at work or at home!

Have a Plan for Both Individual and Team Productivity

If you want your work-from-home policy to work, get very clear about your desired outcome for both individuals and teams. Figure out and make a list of what things the team must work on together, and figure out and make a list of what things will be optimized by individuals working from home. Establish clear desired outcomes, schedules, and priorities both for the individuals and the team.

Once you do this, you can start to create your work-from-home plans and policies. Never just suggest (or tolerate) a work-from-home policy before determining what the business is trying to accomplish, and what teams need to do and what individuals need to do—specifically. And if you are trying to bring a geographically dispersed team and remote working individuals with you through the long Middle of a transformation, you need to be really clear about what you want.

What Does the Team Need?

Have your team work together to define clear team goals. What things does the team need to work on together as a team? How often? What does the team need to learn as a team?

Then, plan and structure in-person meetings and office days around achieving those specific outcomes. Team time is important for collaboration and idea generation. It's important for problem solving and process improvements. Team time is also important to have unstructured discussions about what people are worried about, answer questions, and calm uncertainty. If you are driving change, transformation, or a new strategy, it will never happen if too many people are working from home in an ad-hoc manner.

What Do Individuals Need?

Productivity comes from quality work time on clearly defined outcomes. If you define clear desired outcomes for content, schedule, and quality, and an employee delivers, it should not matter where they do the work. If you've given an individual clear direction on required outcomes and defined stretch goals, you never have to make a personal judgment about whether someone is working hard or slacking off. Either the expectations were met or they were not.

Approve Specific Work-from-Home Days

One mistake I see companies make is to have a work-at-home policy, and then let employees decide on a day-to-day basis when they come in and when they stay home. This does not work. Designate specific work-at-home days for specific people and optimize having the right people in the office at the right times. Require pre-approval for specific work-at-home days vs. people having the expectation that they can just send an email on any given day saying, "I'm working at home today."

Once you do this, you can always expect that the team will be together on certain days of the week for team meetings and collaboration, and that the work-at-home days were chosen with a strategy to optimize individual productivity without sacrificing necessary team time.

Don't confuse achieving business outcomes with giving perks. Do each separately and on purpose.

Consider Mondays

Monday can be a great day for people to take advantage of undistracted thinking and planning time away from the office.

You can have a staff phone call first thing on Monday mornings. Then you can kick off the week and reiterate strategic priorities and specific expectations. Then people can get a less chaotic and more purposeful start to the week, instead of just getting immediately swept into the stream of tactical activities.

Providing Flexibility Is a Good Thing

One of the reasons people like working at home is that they feel in control and they feel trusted. That is good for productivity. They also save loads of time and avoid the mental stress and drain of a commute. I am a big believer in treating people like humans (not "resources") and acknowledging that they have a life that matters outside of work. If you give people schedule flexibility to deal with daily daycare drop-offs and pick-ups and school events, or allow them time away to care for sick family, in my experience they become much more motivated, loyal, and productive. Once you cover the necessary team time when everyone must be together in the office, people will move mountains for you when you really need them to if you don't force them to be in the office all the time, when it doesn't really matter, especially if the performance objectives are defined really clearly. See also Chapter 28: Power and Trust.

MOTIVATING VIRTUAL TEAMS

Okay, so what if your team is *never* in the same room? These days, it is actually quite rare to have a whole team that works in the same building. So how do you create a sense of team, drive productivity, and motivate people you can't spend time with in person?

Virtual Team Building (Literally)

I used to think that team building exercises needed to be reserved for the times when I could get my team in a room together—that with a remote, virtual team, it wasn't possible. But I was pleased to learn the error in that thinking, because remote team building is very possible and can be very effective.

How to Do Remote Team Building

First, prepare. Schedule a team building webinar, video chat, or conference call. Distribute a template ahead of time that each person fills out to share some interesting, personal, non-work stuff about themselves. Create a template that works for your team and culture. Here are some ideas:

- What is your favorite place to spend time outside of where you live?
- What was your best/worst job ever?
- What are your hobbies? Share a photo.
- What is your favorite book, movie, sport, or animal?
- What is something that happened in your childhood that has stayed with you and impacts how you work?
- Show a photo of how you celebrate your favorite holiday in your country.

Then when you have your virtual team building meeting, each person can talk about their template. It is an amazing way to help your team get to know each other as people, and build a much more productive working relationship.

Let's face it, conference calls are painful enough, but conference calls with virtual strangers that only ever talk about work products and responsibilities are not very motivating. But if you take some time to help people get to know each other as people, you can increase motivation and productivity substantially when the team needs to reach across geographies to work together.

Photos! Photos go a long way to build trust and camaraderie. If your team is comfortable with photos, create an internal social sharing page for your team (like a Facebook page) and encourage them to share non-work photos and updates with each other. Photos can sometimes get a little difficult culturally. I've found that if someone refuses to submit a photo, let it go. Don't force the issue.

Improve the Quality of Communications

Another issue with virtual teams is often that they are spread around the world, in different countries with different native languages. Conference call communication is difficult enough, but if it's not in your native language, it's excruciating.

Use Writing in Parallel with Social Media

My friend and colleague, Suzanne Pherigo, created a brilliant process to deal with this. (You may know Suzanne from Azzarello Group FOR-WARD Program Webinar fame, as my co-host). Suzanne runs an international R&D organization. On all of her multi-country conference calls they use an additional IM window where people in each country type out the key points being made, translate any jargon, highlight questions and decisions, and clarify areas in the discussion that were moving fast or unclear.

They also use blog updates that capture the key ideas and decisions from the conference call in writing to reinforce the key outcomes. The blog also automatically creates a record of the conversation and decisions for later review and understanding. This improved both productivity and relationships dramatically. By the way, these are good practices even if there are not language issues!

Have Better Virtual Meetings

We've all been on these virtual team conference calls where most people are checked out and doing email. It's painful and it's a waste of time. I think it's important to be purposeful about having better meetings even when no one is in the room. Here's how I do it: When people are in a meeting I expect them to be *present*—listening, participating, contributing, and *not* doing email. Because if people are not going to be present in a meaningful way, why have a meeting?

> **Insist on starting on time.** Everyone is to call in five minutes prior and be ready to go on time. If need be, start the meeting at five minutes after the hour—sharp! No excuses. Being late degrades accountability for presence and is a huge time waster. Don't tolerate it.

> **Start with a weather report** from each and every person on the call. This gives every person's presence a chance to be felt even though you can't see any of them around the table. And

it gives you an opportunity to treat each person like an individual, which always helps.

Insist that no one mutes their phone. I don't care if I hear children or dogs. Leaving lines unmuted also makes it harder to type, or pursue other distractions without getting found out. Muting lines degrades presence. And it's another big time waster—after a discussion has gone down the road a bit, someone will chime in and say, "Sorry, I didn't realize my phone was on mute and I need to go back to . . ."

Be there. Make it clear that if this is an important meeting, you are supposed to have it on your schedule, be on a landline, and not be driving somewhere. (Driving/traveling should be a pre-approved exception if during an important meeting, not a habit.) You need to set the example for this yourself, too—or don't have the meeting.

Have a clear desired outcome and the promise of a shorter meeting. "Our goal is to achieve this specific outcome in this meeting. We will finish this meeting at 9:45 so that you can hang up and do 15 minutes of something else before your next meeting."

Reinforce the fact that you value each other's time. "The reason we have a shorter meeting, keep our phones un-muted, and don't do email is because we respect each other's time and therefore commit to being present, even though we are not in the same room."

Of course, you can't police this better behavior, but I find that when I express these intentions, more people are truly present and you have a better meeting. Also, if everyone is committed to being present and participating, the meeting is far less boring and more useful. The value of the meeting reinforces the value of the good behaviors.

ADVICE FOR THE REMOTE INDIVIDUAL

If you are a remote leader trying to exert your influence on the business, you can feel invisible, isolated, and disempowered. And no one can see how truly impressive you are in your slippers. Any leader needs to make their presence felt—in the room or from afar. I get these questions so often: "I'm now working remotely, how do I build my brand? How do I influence? How do I develop and maintain sponsorship?"

Exert Your Presence from Afar

If you want to build credibility and influence, you need to do things on purpose to build up and maintain your personal presence. It's harder as a remote employee, but not impossible. Here are some ideas.

1. **Face time first**

   Okay, let's start with the reality. There is no complete substitute for face time. Every time I have had a remote assignment or managed a remote employee I required a two- to four-week break-in period where the person begins the assignment in the office with the team.

   If you "live" with people for a while first, you'll do much better later.

   When you build up some social comfort with each other, then remote is not nearly as distant.

   I would not accept a remote assignment if this was not how it began. With travel budgets frozen it's not always possible to spend time with the people you work with. If travel budgets are frozen, consider footing the bill for your air travel yourself. Find someone to stay with. Tell your manager that you are going to be in town for personal reasons (at no expense to the company) and that you'd like to work at the main office for a couple of weeks while you are there. This is a very worthwhile investment you can make in your career.

   After you get the face time, you will be so much more effective and respected forever after. So if you can establish the face time first, that's great; it's a first step. But then you still need to do the things I describe next to continue to exert your presence. These additional ideas are even more important if you don't have face time first.

2. **Don't hide on conference calls**

   Don't dial in five minutes late, do your email, and not speak. I see this behavior as a habit of remote employees. *People don't see me so it doesn't matter. I'll just stay in the background and get my other work done.* Instead, exert your presence. Dial in five minutes early. Greet everyone who joins. Make sure they know you are there.

I knew a guy who worked remotely who took a picture of himself every day, and whenever he was on a conference call with the group at headquarters, he would email the picture of himself with a note that said something like, "Thought you would want to see what shirt I was wearing today." It may sound silly, but he was exerting his presence. He was well known and respected. And people considered and thought about him. They did not forget he was there.

Exert your presence in words too. Tell them about what it is like where you are at and what you have been working on. Then don't check out during the call. Participate, interrupt, and contribute. Make your presence felt.

3. **Use video**

    I have to say that I am blown away by how much better video calls are for connecting with people than just phone calls. I have clients around the world who I have never met in person, but after a few hours of conversation over video, I feel like they are colleagues and new friends that I truly know personally. If I were a remote employee, I would encourage all of my key colleagues and stakeholders to take a video call with me as often as possible, so we could connect face to face. It makes a huge difference.

4. **Video mail**

    If you can't arrange a video call, try sending a video mail once in awhile. There are many apps that allow for video mail. It's easy and it's free. If you don't have an app handy, google "free video email" to find options. A 30-second video can exert way more presence, be more persuasive, and save both parties more time, than a bunch of email.

5. **Lead things**

    Step forward when things need to get done. Take the lead. Put yourself in the center of a project even though you are not there. Of course it needs to be something you can succeed at remotely, but don't fail to ever take the lead just because you are remote. *If you want to be more relevant—be more relevant!*

6. **Network more**

   Don't wait for people to find and notice you. Be the one to exert your presence, build relationships, share information, and engage. You can build a strong personal brand, even if you are not there. As a remote employee you miss the company lunches and the discussions around the coffee machine. But you don't need to miss connecting with people. Identify people in the company you need to have a relationship with, and build a relationship with them. You should spend at least two hours a week (if not a bit more) just connecting and talking with people at your company. Live connections = presence.

   Reach out to people. Get to know them as people beyond the work discussions. Learn what they care about and enjoy. Contribute things of interest. Where you have key relationships with people, invite them to connect with you on Facebook. Keep yourself current and present in their thinking. When you become a full picture of a person, you have far more presence and are far more visible than when you are just a voice and a work conversation.

7. **Share your ideas and knowledge**

   Become a thought leader in your area of expertise. Consider writing an internal blog. Share interesting news that people at corporate don't see. Seek out external information relevant to your business and be the one to share it. Have a point of view. *Just because you are remote doesn't mean you need to be invisible.* It doesn't mean you can't be a thought leader and have influence on the direction of your business.

NEXT

How will you get everyone in your organization to truly care about the strategy and be invested on a personal level?
   Read on . . .

CHAPTER 15

Getting People to Actually Care

Engagement and Context

As we end Part 2: O = Organization, think about your team and their personal motivation to MOVE.

Once you have the right organization structure, it's important to get people on board and personally motivated to go forward. Even if theoretically all the ropes are tight, if no one wants to start running forward when you release the brake, you'll all just sit there!

WHAT EVERYONE IS THINKING

I'd like to feel like my work matters more.

IF PEOPLE DON'T CARE ON A PERSONAL LEVEL, THEY WON'T *MOVE*

When you are thinking about what it will take to get and keep people moving, it's important to remember that money is not the strongest motivator—meaning is. Don't get me wrong. If you want to change behavior, it certainly doesn't hurt to pay people differently. But if you don't create meaning for people on an individual level, they will not have any personal motivation to move your strategy forward, which is more powerful than money. If you can make people feel that their work is meaningful, you can unlock a tremendous amount of power in your organization.

The Dreaded Mission Statement

Here is where it often goes awry. With all good intentions, management teams who want to create meaning to motivate people to engage decide to put effort into creating a "mission statement." You are probably already rolling your eyes somewhat if you have PTSD from a past mission statement effort.

The creation of a mission statement can become one of the most draining, irritating time wasters in which you can engage a management team. It often results in a statement that reads something like:

> To be the leading provider of the most innovative and high-quality products in our space, with outstanding customer service, and the most efficient operations, therefore maximizing shareholder value.

Okay employees . . . now, hop to it! (Yeah, right.)

The Trick Is That *You* Actually Have to Care

If you want a mission that employees care about, it starts with you actually caring about something.

The employees will never care if the leaders don't. When I work with management teams on this, we start with the questions, "What do you personally care about? Why are you here? What do you admire most about your favorite companies? Why? What things do some businesses do that make you angry? How is it important to treat customers? Employees? Why?" We focus on what the leaders genuinely think and care about first.

This exercise is important because if the leaders don't align on something they authentically care about, it will be impossible to define a mission that the employees can care about on a personal level. If you want your team to be motivated, it starts with you as a leader showing your own excitement and commitment. Your employees will always care more about rising to a higher level of excellence if you show them what you truly care about and why it's personally important to *you* to operate at this level of excellence.

I have found over and over again, in good times and bad, that sharing with employees how I feel personally about the mission at hand gives them permission to feel things too: excited, worried, tired, insecure, confident . . . real feelings. Only when employees are allowed to feel real feelings can they engage personally.

You don't need to specifically call something a mission statement (and you might be better off if you don't!), but you do need to stand for something and care about something for real if you want people to truly engage, to be motivated to spring into action, to run forward and solve problems for you when you release the brake.

What If You Don't Care?

What if you don't really care about your work or your company? What if you are only there because you need the paycheck? Remember, while they are paying you, it is your job to lead, so it is your job to find something you can care about.

If you don't like the product, then care about the way the company treats people. If you don't care about the company, care about the customers.

I've been there. Believe me. It's better to find something to care about than it is to check out. You are way more likely to get yourself into a better job (and maintain your sanity) if you keep caring about something along the way.

CREATE CONTEXT AND MEANING

As we talked about the value of unstructured conversation in Chapter 12, **there is no way to truly engage an employee unless you engage them in a personal way.**

A lot of businesses miss this and treat engagement as a structured, managed program, instead of taking the time and effort to learn what people care about and engage them on a personal level. Employee motivation is not a task you can accomplish with a program; it is an *outcome* of making genuine connections with people.

Make Every Job Matter

Because meaning is the strongest motivator to drive personal engagement, I always make time in my schedule to talk to individuals and mid-level managers to understand how they feel about their jobs. I learn what parts of the business and external world they can (and can't) see from where they sit. Then, I connect the rest of the dots for them.

I do this in one-on-ones, talking with people in the cafeteria, in breakfast meetings, riding in the car for sales calls, brown-bagging it, attending staff meetings of the managers who work in my organization, and taking any other opportunity that comes up.

If you make an effort to share with people how their work fits into the bigger picture, their work will take on a bigger meaning and they will be more motivated and more effective.

There is no better way to have employees understand why their jobs matter than for you to connect the dots for them, and give them a clear line of sight both to the top of the organization and to the outside customer. If you can't explain why each job in your organization matters, you need to question whether or not you need that job in the first place.

Employees who know why their work matters do a better job.

Once people truly understand how their job contributes to the business, they are more likely and able to step up, solve more problems, and add more value.

Taking time to share with every group how the company makes money, where the revenue comes from, and where the profit comes from motivates people to step up and do more for the business.

Helping them understand how the P&L works, and if their jobs are part of the P or the L, and how their jobs impact revenue and profit, makes a big difference not only to morale, but to cost reduction, creative thinking, and innovation.

As a manager, taking the time to think through every role on your team and to create a story and map for how each job impacts the bottom line of the business is an excellent exercise for both you and your team.

Here are a few examples:

Product development. I would explain to my product development organization how we made money and where the revenue came from and where the profit came from. I would explain how getting new products out sooner would benefit not only our competitiveness, but also cost less—and how making it cost less benefited our competitiveness even more. I'd help them understand how their salaries fit into the P&L, and give them ideas of the kinds of things they could do to impact profits by helping sales (make it easier to demo) or reducing expenses (make it easier to test, make it easier to support).

Tech writers. I would give tech writers a chance to interact with customers and share the business model of our customer support function with them. I'd have them talk with customer support people. They would realize that if they could improve the product documentation, it would result in both a better customer experience and a lower support cost. And increased competitiveness.

IT department. I would explain the business model to the IT department and how much each sales rep needed to sell, and what all the steps are in the sales process. I'd tell them about the length of sales cycles and how special deals were often given in the last 24 hours of the month. That would help them to understand why the IT systems had to carry a heavier load (and needed to stay available and working!) at those times. They'd realize that they could change the way they planned and managed IT services to support the sales team, to make closing business and handling special pricing easier.

When people feel like their job matters, and they understand the big picture and how the P&L works, they have the motivation, the context, and the insight to truly engage and to come up with innovative ideas that benefit the bottom line.

NEXT

It's a long journey through the Middle, and you need to stay strong, personally motivated, and focused when countless things that will come up challenge and distract you. You need to be brave. You need to be persistent.. You need to stay focused. So the next part of the model is about you. And it is about Valor!

Read on . . .

PART 3

V = Valor

Facing the Hardest Stuff with Courage and Persistence

If you are going through hell—keep going!
—Winston Churchill

E ven with the best plans and the best team, the Middle is long and there will be many obstacles and setbacks. There will be skepticism, lethargy, and disagreements. There will be urgent demands, opportunities, and crises that will tempt you to stop the strategic work you are doing and react. You need to have the valor to stick to your strategy through the whole Middle every day, with every behavior and every decision.

CHAPTER 16

Mission Impossible

Dealing with Obstacles, Fear, and Imposter Syndrome

WHAT EVERYONE IS THINKING

I'm afraid that I'm not good enough.

If you are human, you will be afraid sometimes. If you are a leader, you will be attacked and challenged sometimes. At times your job will feel so ugly and impossible that you think you will surely fail. In my experience, the bigger the job, the harder it gets because as you move higher, there is less clarity of expectations, less support from your direct manager, less feedback, and higher stakes. There is also much more competition for budget, people, and charter.

That brings us to Part 3: V = Valor because leadership is hard. That's why you need Valor to progress through the long Middle.

WELCOME TO BEING A LEADER

I can remember feeling at various points in my career that the mission just didn't make sense, or that it was unsupported. I felt like I was out on a limb owning all of the risk, and with not enough resources to succeed. Or I felt like the corporate bureaucracy, the board, or another group or particular adversary was blocking me (or sabotaging me) from doing the right things that I knew needed to be done. Or I would get a directive that didn't make any sense like, "You must cut costs by 50 percent but you can not make any cuts to the biggest program."

As a leader, this unreasonable, soul-crushing stuff is just part of the job description. There are always big, ugly, seemingly impossible problems, annoying people, and exhausting obstacles in the way of getting your job done. And when you are leading, by definition you are going to a place where others aren't. You are embarking on new territory, which can be scary and lonely.

Think of Valor in this way:

Once you embrace the fact that your job = your job description plus all the crap that gets in the way of delivering on your job description . . . you will feel (and be) in a lot more in control.

I coach a lot of senior executives and with pretty much everyone we reach a point where I tell them, "You'll be better off if you start your thinking with this: **Everything is impossible and everyone is a shark.** That's just the way it is. And it's your job to deal with that." Usually that makes people feel better because they can let go of the idea that it is about them personally, and they can step back, see the problem more clearly, and treat it like any other challenge.

If you can get your head around the fact that everything is supposed to be hard or nearly impossible, and that you are likely to be swimming with predators, you can start using the same talents and energy that you use to solve sensible business problems to address these personal challenges too. It's possible to treat this type of obstacle like any other project or program and get busy working to overcome it.

If instead you spend energy thinking, *But this is totally unreasonable and others are out to get me*, that line of thinking (while it might be true) doesn't give you an action plan to deal with it. Waiting for the rest of the world to get reasonable is a bad strategy because it doesn't happen. As a leader you need to accept this and get to work. Or don't be a leader. Sorry. But it's true.

It's not always quite this brutal. Sometimes it feels more like: My hard work is not recognized, appreciated, or valued. No one gives me feedback. No one cares about me. But if you are a leader, at any level, if it feels hard, it is more a sign that you are doing it right than it is a sign that you are doing it wrong.

FOUR THINGS THAT WILL HELP YOU FEEL LESS CRAZY AND STRESSED

1. It's Okay to Be Scared

First and foremost, I think it's important to say loud and clear that it is okay to be scared.

Everyone is scared.

Every time I took a step forward, started a big new project, or got a big promotion, I was scared. And it was okay. If you are a human, you are going to be scared . . . unless you are a psychopath who has no ability to feel anything. Those are your two choices: scared or psychopath.

Know that everybody is bluffing, at least sometimes. Everyone has moments in their careers when they feel like a fraud or an imposter. It's not just you.

If you feel scared it's because you are challenging yourself and progressing, not because you are not good enough.

One of my favorite authors, Elizabeth Gilbert, describes how she manages her fear in a way that I find incredibly useful. She realized that her fear was never going to go away. So she instead made friends with it. When she needed to face a big challenge, her fear would show up on cue to try and stop her. Instead of trying to deny her fear, or eliminate it, or be paralyzed by it, she would say something like, "Hey fear, it's you again. You are welcome to come along, but you have to sit in the back seat—and you don't get to talk—and you absolutely don't get to drive."

Don't worry that your fear is there. Just accept it and invite it along for the ride. Once you make your fear welcome, it has far less power to stop you from doing things.

As leaders, we need to accept our fear and deal with it in a positive way that lets us move forward. When leaders instead let their fear drive, I see two damaging things happen. One is that the person's fear will cause them to disqualify themselves when they shouldn't, and the other is that unmanaged fear will cause them to treat others badly.

Fear Problem #1: Don't Disqualify Yourself   You think, *That's a great opportunity, but I am not ready for it because it seems so big and scary. And because I'm scared, that must mean I'm not qualified. If I was qualified, I wouldn't be scared.* Wrong. **Scared does not equal not qualified.**

Everyone would be scared by this opportunity. In reality, the people who decide to go for that big opportunity are also scared. The only difference is that they do it anyway.

> **No matter how much you achieve, as soon as you take on the next challenge, it's scary again, and the voice inside your head starts shouting "Imposter! You are not competent enough! You will be found out!" This feeling never goes away.**

Don't let that voice stop you from doing the things you need to do and want to do as a leader and in your life. Sometimes you just need to step forward, take a leap, and trust yourself. You are a smart and capable person, and you will learn the unknown, intimidating stuff as you go. It's okay to be scared, but sometimes when you are scared you need to do it anyway. That is a big part of Valor.

Fear Problem #2: Treating Others Badly   I think so much of the dysfunction in business is rooted in leaders being scared and insecure. When leaders are scared and insecure, they can resort to micro-managing; become bullies; withdraw from honest, unstructured communication; refuse to hire or support really smart people . . . the list goes on and on.

It's so important to accept your fear and deal with it in a positive and productive way so that it does not cause you to either sabotage or disqualify yourself or treat others badly.

2. Do What Is True for You

In my own career my fear manifested itself for years as insecurity about my young age. I wasted so much time and energy making sure that no one found out how young I was. When I became a general manager for the first time at age 33, I was deeply invested in my fear of being too young and the associated imposter syndrome of getting such a big job at that age. Surely someone was going to find out how young I was and say, "You are not allowed to have this job!"

Also at times I was in very male-dominated and/or very technology-dominated environments. I was told I was not technical enough, and through words and dismissive behaviors, that I was not [man enough] or welcome. I was just this young woman who did not deserve a seat at the table.

Before I started my first GM job, I got some advice from an executive coach, an HR manager, and a media coach. They all told me the same thing: "Patty, give up this older act. You are actually much more credible and powerful when you allow yourself to be your true self. When you are too tired to keep up this facade, the real you that comes through is actually much more powerful than this more serious, pretend-to-be-older business person you are trying to be." I see many executives make this same mistake of thinking that to build credibility, their real self is actually not good enough in some way, so they decide to project a more executive-like persona. But the problem is that this persona ends up being a false one. And you simply can't build as much credibility, confidence, and trust if you are being false, no matter how much better you think your managed identity is than your real self.

So when I started in my new GM role, I did exactly what they suggested. I was myself. I didn't broadcast how old I was, but I didn't hide it either. I led with my strengths, and I let my full personality shine through. I had unstructured conversations with all of my direct reports and people in my organization without fear that they would "find me out." The result was great.

It was really scary to let go of my managed, older persona at first because I felt like exposing the real me left me, well, exposed. But what I realized is that by showing up as my authentic self, I earned credibility and respect far more quickly than ever before. No one made an issue of my age. Ever. It was such a more impactful way to behave, and it required far less energy.

People can see authentic—and it is a powerful thing. You are always your most powerful when you are being authentic. You can't fake being authentic!

Think about the people you see and interact with. When someone is being authentic, you can tell. You notice it. It's like a certain kind of light is shining. It's obvious. It's inspiring. Being authentic as you show up each day throughout the Middle is so important for others because it also builds tremendous confidence and trust. Trust is a necessary enabler to keep everyone moving forward. See also Chapter 28: Power and Trust.

Find a Core Truth to Confront a Challenge or Attack   When you are in a challenging situation and you feel scared, your authentic self can come to the rescue here too. Your best strategy to confront a difficult challenge or attack that is making you feel really scared, insecure, or uncomfortable is to find a place of core truth to operate from. As soon as you do you will feel more powerful, more effective, and less nervous. You will be supporting yourself instead of judging or criticizing yourself. You will think, *Because I really believe this, I know this to be true, I know this is right for me—if I start from here, it will be okay.*

When everything feels impossible and everyone seems like a shark, instead of getting nervous or frustrated, assert yourself—your true self. And that comfort will turn into confidence that will allow you to show up with strength. Whenever I talk to a leader about the toughest times in their careers and how they dealt with it, it always comes back to them finding something that was true for them, and using that to regain their footing, and ultimately their confidence and success.

For example, when I was being dismissed as not being technical enough, instead of being defensive about it and trying to find a way to be, or to project being more technical, I decided to stay true to myself. The environment was loaded with highly technical people. So I said, "You are quite right, I am not as technical as you. But the last thing you need here is another one of you! There are enough technical people here. You need *me* to be here and to be different than you. You need someone with strategic business thinking skills and sales and marketing experience—someone like me to bring your technology into the world in a way that people will buy it. You don't want or need me to be more technical. You need me to be what I am and to do what I do." That was a place of truth for me where I could feel stronger and less defensive. I immediately felt better. They not immediately, but eventually, backed off and came to appreciate my different, authentic contribution.

3. Use Mentors and Experts

I can't imagine trying to survive any leadership role without mentors. To me it's like attempting to climb Mt. Everest without a Sherpa and a guide. Sure you could try. But why on Earth would you?

When I felt really stuck, I was always so grateful to have mentors I could go to who cared about me, and who could help me see the things I wasn't seeing and find a way forward. Mentors are so necessary, not only to ask for help when you need it, but also to point out your blind spots—the things that can kill you and you didn't even see coming. I've written extensively about mentors on my blog and in my first book *RISE*. As a leader, it's vital that you have at least one mentor who is 10 to 15 years your senior who sees all of your biggest, soul crushing problems as "been there, done that, got the T-shirt," and can tell you about the important things you don't know about yet.

The Accidental Expert   Another downfall I see that fear causes among leaders is that it makes them afraid to ask for help. Asking for help does not make you appear weak; it actually makes you more credible . . . because you get help! You get smarter. And the people who help you see you getting smarter because they can see you learning from them.

> **It's always important to remember that the most successful people are the ones who get the most help.**

One of my favorite examples of this is when, early into my first general management role, my team had identified a significant gap in our product offering, and the recommendation was that we acquire a technology from another company to fill the gap. Although I totally understood and agreed with the business and technical rationale for this, I had not the faintest idea of how to do a deal like this.

We were not just buying the product or setting up a partnership; we wanted to acquire the technology outright. This was a deal that was going to include things like stock warrants and term sheets and lawyers. (Honestly, at the time I did not even know what a warrant or a term sheet was!) I went through something like the phases of grief:

#1. I'm going to get fired . . .

My first thought was panic . . . game over—I'm going to get found out. I'm going to get fired. I'm too young. I don't have enough experience. A general manager should know how to do this. All of my peers are making deals like this. Once people find out I don't know how to do this, I'm going to get fired because I don't deserve to be a general manager.

#2. Get a grip

After a few hours of panicking, I came to my senses and thought, "Patty, you work for a big company. Surely there is someone here who knows how to do this! Go get help."

#3. Ask the experts

After a couple of phone calls, I made my way to the corporate development department—and they were so glad I showed up! I described the business situation, and before I knew it, I had a team of experts educating me about what I needed to know. They gave me a list of questions and negotiating points to ask the CEO of the target company, and they created a term sheet for me. (And they told me what a term sheet was!)

I sheepishly took my brand-new knowledge and stack of agreements and proposals into the meeting with the CEO. I followed the script exactly. We made a deal.

(Just as an aside, in this very scary situation, the truth I found for myself that let me move forward, as we discussed previously, was this: *I know that I can get help and learn fast. I don't need to know everything. I can trust myself to do something new and difficult as long as I get help with the content.*)

The Real Punchline of This Story

The punchline of the story is that as a result of that deal, I became known as the best dealmaker in the group.

How ridiculous is that? Going from thinking I am going to get fired for something I don't know how to do, to being known as the person who is the best at it—in one step! It turned out that while my peers where all wheeling and dealing on their own, as smart and impressive and intimidating as they looked to me, they were making bad deals for the company. My deal was accretive. It didn't expose us in any unnecessary way. It had back outs. It had upsides. It was a good deal.

One important lesson I took from this was a reinforcement of something I strongly believe—never fail alone. There is always someone to ask for help. Never let your ego get in the way of asking for help.

But the big, life-changing "aha" moment for me was this: I can be even more successful doing something that I *don't* know how to do than doing something I *do* know how to do because if I know how to do it, I'll be inclined to just do it myself. So I'll be limited to my own knowledge. But if I don't know how to do it, I will ask for help and get the benefit of experts!

So Why Not Always Ask the Experts for Help? Asking for help when you feel like you need it is always a great thing to do. But asking for help from experts even when you don't feel like you need it can make the difference between simply getting something done and creating huge success. Since this time, I have forced myself to create a new habit of always seeking input from smart people and experts. It's always worth getting smarter! And you may become an accidental expert like I did, when you make it a habit of learning from the best.

4. The Parallel Universe Exercise

When I find myself feeling very discouraged and out of moves, in an "everything is impossible and everyone is a shark" situation, I do what I refer to as my "parallel universe" thought exercise. I imagine that a parallel universe exists that replicates the same situation exactly.

In that universe, all the same problems and pressures are there. All the same people are there. Everything about the situation is exactly the same—except there is a version of me in that parallel universe that is better and more capable than me in every conceivable way. The parallel universe Patty is smarter. She is a faster thinker, better problem solver, better negotiator, better communicator, and better networker. She is more experienced, kinder, braver, and has better hair.

The parallel universe Patty always has more energy than I do to keep fighting, and offers a new angle to try. So next time you feel thoroughly discouraged and stuck, ask yourself, *In a parallel universe, that is exactly the same as this, but has a better version of me: What would that better version of me do?* **The "Patty with the better hair" always instructs me to step up and be better and braver in some specific way that will help.**

The parallel universe Patty has never failed to help me come up with an idea to get un-stuck, feel less victimized, and start moving forward. She always provides new and better thinking. She encourages me to try stuff. She shows me how to be braver. She shows me Valor.

It's Hard to Stick to a Transformation Through the Long Middle

As you read the next chapters in Part 3: V = Valor, think about your personal leadership strategy and use these ideas as tools to develop your confidence. Keep your transformation on track by being very consistent and helping your team deal with their own fear, doubts, and skepticism.

The Middle is hard. It's scary. People will fight you either outwardly or with passive aggressive inaction. Expect it.

Use these tools to stick to your strategic program through the Middle when the tactical pressures of the moment and the current workload become overwhelming. Use these tools when the old way of doing things starts to pull everyone back, and you are tempted to second-guess your strategic investment or give up.

It's okay to be scared. That's why you need Valor.

Next

The Middle will be full of challenges, attacks, skepticism, and a very strong pull to go back to the old way. You need Valor to keep everyone moving forward when people start trying to run back.
    Read on . . .

CHAPTER 17

Burn the Ships at the Beach

How to Keep Moving Forward When No One Wants To

WHAT EVERYONE IS THINKING

Can we please stop doing this? I don't see the benefit. It's not working. In fact, it's harming the business. We need to go back to the old way!

I've said it before and I'll keep saying it. The Middle is long. This long amount of time allows for so many opportunities for people to question the strategy and the tactics, and to pick apart pretty much anything you are trying to change. The new stuff is hard, and may in some ways be unpleasant. People's favorite projects might have been canceled or delayed. New skills are required. The payoff is not obvious yet. People want to go back to the old way, because the old way is familiar. It's comfortable. It's easier: "This new thing . . . well . . . it just isn't working."

"BURN THE SHIPS AT THE BEACH"

First, a brief historical reference: 1519 AD, during the Spanish conquest of Mexico, Hernán Cortés, the Spanish commander, scuttled his ships so that his men would have to conquer or die, no matter how hard the mission became and how much they might have wanted to turn back. There was no turning back because the ships were gone. Forward was the only choice.

This was a phrase I learned from my boss in one of my roles, when I was asked to step in to run a software development organization of about 200 people. In this situation my boss taught me a lot about Valor. He had it. He required me to step up and have it too.

When I got there the team was on a two-year product development cycle— and we were running late! The quality of our product was very low, and the morale of the organization was even lower. The sales force and customers had abandoned us. It was a mess.

Our strategy for the business became to fix the quality problems *and* get on a predictable software development and release schedule. The bulk of executing this landed on me. We adopted, at the direction of my boss, a process framework called the SEI process, which is a predefined software development process with rules and checkpoints that occur at each step in a software development program. SEI process improvement became our "ruthless priority" for the year. (See Chapter 18: Too Busy to Scale, for more on ruthless priorities.)

This was not an easy ask of the organization.

Software developers are enormously talented and creative people who can work miracles. But as a group what they do not love is a process improvement initiative! My boss's mantra for our organization was "process, schedule, features." Process was the priority, because that was what was going to improve our quality and predictability and allow us to turn the business around and get the sales force and customers back. The priorities that software developers prefer are features, features, features. We were putting the only thing they cared about last. This was not an easy sell.

Now I'm not a lover of process for process' sake, but I am for just enough process to make things better. To give you a sense of what we were doing, we were going from SEI Level 1, which was defined as "chaos," to SEI Level 2, which is defined as "managed." There are five levels. All I needed was to get us to Level 2. Level 2 basically says that you are no longer in chaos. Level 2 requires that you must commit to what you are going to do and write it down. If you want to change what you committed, you have to go through a change review process, document the change, and write it down. For each phase in the process there is a checklist that you go through to make sure you completed all the work, communication, and review necessary to move from one phase to the next. This was not an overwrought or detailed process. This was simply going from "chaos" to "managed."

The way that this played out was, after rolling out the process framework and checkpoint lists and committing to the feature set for our next release, on any given day, when a sales person or a customer said, "I must have this feature now," an engineer would come to me and say, "I need to add this feature." I would say, "Process, schedule, features: Does adding this feature at this time go against our defined process? Does adding this feature impact our committed schedule?"

The engineers absolutely hated this. The other thing they would try to do to get around the annoying process work would be to try to blackmail me and say something like, "I can finish this on time, but not if I have to fill out these process documents. If I have to do all this extra process work, then I am going to be late." I would say: "Process, schedule, features: I want this to be on time, so do your best, but you can't skip the process work. It's a must, and it's a higher priority than schedule, so please complete it."

I would go to my boss and say, "This is really hard, everybody hates this, and they argue with me every day." And he would say to me, "Patty, you have to burn the ships at the beach." He taught me that you have to make it very clear at the beginning of a difficult journey that there is no turning back. The only way through is forward. If you go back, there is nothing there for you. You can't get back.

And he taught me that the way you "burn the ships at the beach" is to be completely consistent in your message and your decisions.

People would tell me, "You are being stupid, you are killing our business, we're going to lose our top people over this," and I'd say, "I understand your frustration, but this is what we are doing, and I am committed to it. I promise you in the long run it will be good for the business."

Then they would get very upset and go to my boss and say, "Patty is killing the business, this process stuff is wasting time, and we are not going to be competitive if we don't put this feature in."

He would reply: "Process, schedule, features."

To jump to the end, as soon as we got on this process, we reduced our cycle time from two years to six months. We did our first release nine months after we launched the process and did the next two releases like clockwork six and twelve months after that. The quality improved dramatically. We lost two top engineers who were just too angry that they couldn't do exactly as they pleased, but the morale of the rest of the team skyrocketed. (People love to finish things.) We were able to re-recruit a sales force and win the customers back. The engineers realized that shorter, predictable cycles allowed them to be even more creative and that they could make better choices because we were getting real market feedback on finished products that were out in the market. They never loved the process part, but they ultimately admitted that it helped, and they became personally committed to it.

I was so proud of this accomplishment and this team because we began to operate like a well-oiled, predictable machine. You could give us any task, and we'd run it through this process and get it done. But it was *so* hard to get to that point. It required standing up to criticism, doubt, and attacks every single day for months. I doubted myself many times when a new feature seemed really urgent and important. But I stuck to the process, and it had a huge payoff. I learned so many lessons about Valor from this experience:

1. Say what you mean and defend it.
2. Don't change your mind.
3. Guard the people who are doing the right thing with your life.
4. Pick one thing at a time.
5. Don't lose your nerve.
6. Don't get bored or tired.

Let me say more about each of these things.

Say What You Mean and Defend It

The first step is to really mean what you say. I truly believed that we would be better off with predictable schedules and higher quality than we would be by remaining on the course we were on. I communicated that I cared about this transformation and that I was truly in it. I had their back. I assured them that we were not going to get in trouble for following this strategy. I reminded them about this weekly if not daily. If you need to drive a transformation or achieve a strategic initiative, you actually have to care about it personally. If you don't, you'll never be able to stand up to the resistance through the long Middle. See also Chapter 15: Getting People to Actually Care.

Don't Change Your Mind

Your organization will be watching for the slightest pause or gap in your commitment. If they see it, it's game over. You are hedging; you've left a ship on the beach after all. They've got you. They'll go back. When people run back to the beach, you have to make sure that they see that there are no ships—there is no way back. So their only choice is to turn around and move forward again. Once you commit to the way forward, you as the leader have to stay truly committed. When short-term crises or opportunities and shiny objects come up, you need to resist reacting to them.

Guard the People Who Are Doing the Right Thing with Your Life

In every change initiative, there will be someone on your team who is doing what you need. They have resisted the early cultural hesitation, and they are fully engaged in the new work. Guard that person with your life. That person is at very high risk because the naysayers will know that you are unshakeable, but maybe that guy isn't. They will go straight to him and say, "Please work on this other thing that is very urgent." When that guy comes to you and says, "What should I do?" you have a unique opportunity to do a very right or very wrong thing. The right thing to do is to say, "You keep on working on the new thing, I've got this." Then you own the urgent request personally. You either shut it down or find a way to get it done without impacting the new work and squandering the commitment and Valor of your hero. If you shut down the urgent request, you can make it very clear that it was an inappropriate request. It kills me when I see a GM snatch defeat out of the jaws of victory by pulling the one person who is succeeding at the strategic work to respond to the tactical. That is a total failure of Valor. Get it done somehow if you must, but please protect your best ambassador working on the strategic new thing.

Pick One Thing at a Time

Another important thing that I learned is that this is truly the definition of "ruthless" in a "ruthless priority" (see Chapter 18). You simply cannot have this level of fierce support for more than one thing at a time. This doesn't mean that your business can only do one thing, but it means that you can only really protect one thing at a time with this level of ferocity. Think about the one thing that is most important in your business—the one thing that if you don't get right, you'll die. That should be your one ruthless priority, and you should defend it until it's done.

Don't Lose Your Nerve

If it feels nearly impossible, you are doing it right. Any change, transformation, or new initiative will come with a lot of skepticism, disagreement, debate, attack, and passive aggressive shots. Stick with it. When you feel nervous, realize that it's okay to feel nervous, but it's more important to keep moving forward and stick with it. If you let your nerves make you hedge because it seems more comfortable, you are leaving a ship at the beach and your team will find it. You'll go backwards.

Don't Get Bored or Tired

Remember, strategic, long-term initiatives take time! Not only do you have to do all of this hard stuff consistently, you have to do it for a really long time. You might get bored with the continual focus on the same ideas and messages, but realize that your team desperately needs that consistency from you. It's scary for them to leave the beach and face the unknown in the deep woods. They need to feel your support throughout the whole journey through the Middle, not just at the beginning when you are most excited about it. Valor is about patience and persistence too.

Next

The biggest temptation of all is staying too busy with present work to be able to move the new thing forward. How will you choose what to stop doing?
     Read on . . .

CHAPTER 18

Too Busy to Scale

Use Ruthless Priorities to Enable Growth

WHAT EVERYONE IS THINKING

I'm so busy. I don't even have time to think about something new, let alone do something new. I'm focused on revenue. We have customer crises. I don't have time for planning or process or infrastructure. I'm busy on revenue-generating stuff!

The companies that scale are the ones who choose to do less stuff.

It might sound a little counterintuitive, but the companies who scale are the ones who do fewer things. It works because they can do those few things really well. By comparison, the companies who get stuck often get stuck because they keep trying to do too many things. You can't do too many things well. This is another area that requires extreme Valor, because it's really hard to say *no* to opportunities and give up potential or actual revenue streams in order to focus on becoming great at the few things you choose to win at.

As a leader it's vitally important to develop your confidence in this area. Study successful companies. Every chance you get, talk to CEOs of companies who scaled and ask them, "Did you ever have a scary decision where you had to abandon some revenue streams or opportunities in order to focus on winning in fewer markets?" They will always say, "Yes," because **chaos doesn't scale.**

There are three problems related to doing too many things that will keep you in chaos and stall your forward progress.

Problem #1: Addicted to Busy

It's so tempting to stay busy, because, first of all, it's scary to say no, and secondly, being really busy can make people feel heroic and important. Much of the busy stuff can be related directly to bringing in revenue. What could be more important than that? How can that be wrong?

It's wrong because now it's stalling you. You are overwhelmed with work. You are too busy, and it's too chaotic to get the things done that will enable you to scale. Yes, you might have brought in that $3M deal, but you pulled the whole team off the new initiative to do it, so you failed on the effort to open up that new $100M channel. Or you might have needed to do custom work to get that deal, which pulled your key developers off your next $100M product line.

It feels right to keep pursuing every piece of revenue because that has made you successful in the past. It's what successfully got you to $200M. You had to be nimble. You had to be aggressive. You had to make deals happen. You had to drop everything to get that next, big reference customer. You had to stop work on your roadmap to get your biggest deal ever. None of that was the wrong choice at the time. But now that way of working is what's holding you back.

> **You can't even think about scaling to be a $1B company because you are too busy being a $200M company.**

When short-term pressures chronically prevent you from doing more strategic stuff, you end up burning all your time and resources reacting to issues and opportunities in an ad hoc manner, instead of making progress on strategic work that will let you scale. New initiatives require new work. If people are just too busy and distracted to get traction on the new thing, it doesn't get done simply because there is no time to do it.

Another question I ask CEOs is this: "You are a $200M company today. When you are a $1B company do you think that you will operate [a chaotic area in the business] the same way?" They almost always say,

"No, of course not." So then I ask, "Okay, at what point between now and when you are a $1B company do you think you need to start operating in the new way?"

By definition you will need to be doing things differently at $1B than you are doing at $200M. So when do you make the switch?

Hint: you don't get there until after you make the switch.

Think of one of the chaotic areas in your business, and imagine it operating in the same way but with five times more revenue. Could you manage five times more revenue production at the same level and in the same way as you do it now? If one person is handling it now, can you just hire another four people to do it? Maybe . . . but remember, chaos doesn't scale. If you only know how to scale your expenses linear to your revenue growth, you lose. You'll find that if you just grow the chaotic workload as is, you will have other breakdowns in systems and communications. It's just not possible to do it the same way when you get bigger.

In this case Valor is required to break the cycle. You need to change the systems and the approach to create a more streamlined, repeatable infrastructure that can accomplish ten times as much without costing ten times as much.

Here is what I recommend. List all the places in your business where you are too busy. Is it customer support? Is it delivery? Is it a backend process? Pick the one that is causing you the most pain and creating the most wasted energy. Then ask, "How must this work when we grow by ten times?" Start making the change now—in this one area. Fund it. Focus on it. Do it. You don't need to scale everything all at once, but you also can't just wait until you get bigger, because you won't ever get bigger if you don't start scaling.

PROBLEM #2: DOING TOO MANY THINGS

Valor is very much about having the guts to make the choice of doing fewer things. It's much easier in the moment to keep doing too many things than to have the nerve to make the strategic choice of what to stop. This is one of the hardest challenges of being a business leader—and if you are avoiding it, you are in good company. This issue is rampant. I see it everywhere—because it is so hard. You need to make choices and trade-offs. You need to decide where you are going to place your bets and then you need to stop doing some other stuff.

As a leader if you are not waking up every morning thinking about what trade-offs you need to make, you are not doing the job.

The reasons why it requires Valor to make trade-offs and choose to do fewer things are at least twofold. One, you will be disappointing people internally who have been invested in one of the programs that will not move forward. And two, you may need to face your executive management, board, or even Wall Street and say that you are giving up an existing revenue stream to put more focus on a growing revenue stream. You need to have the guts to sell it.

I see a lot of leaders choose the path that requires less Valor in the moment but actually is more risky in the long run. They are so afraid to give up any bit of potential revenue for even a short time that they continue to try to keep doing everything, so nothing ever scales in a material way. But they have avoided the difficult conversations.

I loved Google's founders' IPO letter to shareholders: "As a private company, we have concentrated on the long term, and this has served us well. As a public company, we will do the same. In our opinion, outside pressures too often tempt companies to sacrifice long-term opportunities to meet quarterly market expectations. The Google founders had the Valor to stand up to Wall Street and typical shareholder expectations of quarterly performance. They said we have a long-term view and it's better for everyone.

I have led several successful turnarounds in my career, and I can tell you that the secret to success was to pick one thing to focus on and do it well. It was always remarkable to see how much more functional the organization became after we stopped trying to be bigger than we deserved to be by trying to do too many things. And once we had our focus, it also became much more clear how to scale, because we had eliminated so much complexity.

PROBLEM #3: BEING TOO REACTIVE

Okay. You've made some key decisions. You've made some big trade-offs, and you have focused plans. You're excited about implementing the strategic initiatives that will scale your business. But then, oops, there is a customer emergency. Everyone drops everything, and it's all hands on deck until the customer is satisfied. Strategic work stalls.

Or you might have a team of top people working on market-changing product developments, strategic partnerships, or long-term, integrated, go-to-market initiatives, but then a big deal comes across the table, and they get pulled off this work to do whatever it takes to make sure the deal closes.

It takes tremendous Valor to keep your people working on strategic things. First you have to break free of the thinking that you are always doing the right thing by chasing revenue. Then you have to ask yourself, *Why do we have to do so many, reactive, nonstandard things to win in the first place?*

I worked with one company where one of the founders was responsible for creating the new platform that would allow the company to create repeatable engagements with enterprise clients, vs. having to do custom, time consuming work with every single customer. This was an improvement absolutely fundamental to scaling. But he also happened to be the only expert who could come to the rescue when a vital sales situation or big issue with a customer came up.

So every time a customer emergency came up, he got on an airplane. Two years went by, and he (and the company) had made no progress at all on the most important strategic endeavor.

Can you spot the problem? Without an intentional change to choose strategic over reactive, this situation will never resolve itself. They were locked in a loop that resulted in never solving the core problem. They were allowing the sales force and the founder to remain reactive. Some things they could have done differently:

1. Train more people to do the critical customer work, so the founder wouldn't need to be the one to go every time. To do this, the founder should never go alone; he should always bring someone along to train and get the sales force used to relying on other people.

2. Understand why these customer emergencies were coming up in the first place and resolve the root cause issue.

3. Equip the sales force to sell differently in the first place to avoid getting into these situations, which require heroic effort from the founder to resolve.

4. Get the company aligned on keeping the founder focused on making strategic progress.

Leaders need to start thinking differently about how they should be working. They need to spend more time thinking so they can spend less time reacting.

How to De-Risk the Most Important Actions
What Everyone Is Thinking

We have 11 critical, strategic initiatives. I have them on a laminated card somewhere. I don't remember what they are . . . and by the way, they all have sub-bullets . . .

Ruthless Priorities

I introduced this concept of "ruthless priorities" in my first book *RISE*. Why ruthless priorities are so important for succeeding through the Middle is because they establish the list of non-negotiable things (very few, one to three) that you *refuse to put at risk*. And because it's one to three things, everyone can remember the list.

Prioritizing among your list of already prioritized things is really hard!

All these priorities are super-important. That's why they are priorities. It's impossible to draw a cut line. And generally speaking, even if you get really clear on priorities for a moment, something can happen with a customer or competitor or an internal hiccup that throws your brilliant plan into chaos and forces you to react and re-prioritize. Picking and sticking to ruthless priorities is one of the hardest and most important things that great leaders do. It's what makes them stand out. It's what makes them successful. It's what lets them scale.

The trick I found to picking ruthless priorities is to go through your too-long list of priorities, and instead of asking "How important is this?" **Look at each one of your priorities and ask, "How bad is it if I fail?"**

If I fail, will I be embarrassed about disappointing someone? Will the business stop? Will someone go to jail? Once you start asking, "How bad is it if I fail?" you'll find that true ruthless priorities will emerge.

Then once you have ruthless priorities, it doesn't mean that you completely stop doing everything else. It means fundamentally that **you have declared a few things that you will not put at risk under any circumstances.**

You will do these few things first and best and get them done no matter what. It changes the conversation. It's not that you have to say *no* to everything else; it's that since you have selected one or two things that you will get done no matter what else comes up, to everything else you can say, "Later" or "Less."

Don't schedule 100 percent of capacity on your ruthless priorities since that puts them at risk, because something will always come up. Think about removing all risk on one or two things, and you'll actually get them done!

What I have found is that being clear about ruthless priorities helps your whole organization make in-the-moment trade-offs throughout the Middle when the pressure mounts to react to short-term emergencies. It increases everyone's Valor!

Communicate (a Lot) About Your Ruthless Priorities

It is also vital that you communicate the key work that supports your ruthless priorities. I always had a communication document with me (one page) that listed my ruthless priorities and what the top initiatives were to accomplish them. This list came with me wherever I went and was part of every conversation I had. (Sometimes the dentist didn't care.)

What I found is that the more I communicated what my organization was doing (to other organizations and external parties) and why it was so critical to the business, the more focused my organization became and the less hassle we received to do other things.

If you can explain the business value of your ruthless priorities, it is a wonderful defense against extra work. You can say, "I think you'll agree that we must get [this] done first, because it is so vitally important to the business. I will get to your thing after we finish this." The better you can sell the importance of your ruthless priorities, the more others will back off. Really.

CONFLICTING RUTHLESS PRIORITIES

People can get confused when they find that their ruthless priorities conflict with the ruthless priorities of another group. They need to get cooperation from the other group to support their own ruthless priorities, but the other group says, "I don't have time, your thing is not on *my* list of ruthless priorities." This is a "game over" moment.

If we fast forward through all the good leadership behaviors that these two individuals could demonstrate to work this out between themselves, and they can't work it out, then, in the spirit of keeping things moving forward, both groups should escalate it to their managers and say, "We have a ruthless priority conflict. One of these will be at risk, can you help?" The use of ruthless priorities provides an excellent mechanism to escalate the right stuff.

It's also a beautiful thing to see this work in action. One time I was sitting in the office of a director, and a manager came in and said, "I just got this urgent request from sales. If I do this it will put at risk the ruthless priority that we agreed I was working on, so I wanted to give you a heads up." In this moment the director said, "You keep working on the ruthless priority. I've got your back. I'll take this request and get it handled another way. You need to stay focused." It was a beautiful thing!

NEXT

One of the other things that keep organizations too busy to scale is detail. Learn how to rise above the detail and keep moving forward through the Middle.

Chapter 19

Detail

The Momentum Killer: Manage Outcomes Instead

The Cost of Detail

A big issue I see some leaders struggle with is that they are so addicted to detail that they insist that operational details be dragged up and vetted through every level of management and reviewed and inspected over and over again.

The idea that your value as a leader is only highly regarded if you understand a deep level of detail is a false one. To insist that all of your managers must also stay versed in all the detail kills organizational effectiveness, is hugely expensive, and introduces more risk than it averts. Reviewing detail at every level wastes a huge amount of time (everyone's time)—time that is then not spent on moving the business forward.

As a leader, if you think that your personally examining lots of detail is helping your organization, it isn't.

I see this a lot. Progress grinds to a halt because it takes hours and hours for everyone to review all the detail. By the time it gets to the executive, dozens of people at multiple levels have reviewed the detail, but no one has had any time to do anything about it!

One big reason for executive attention to detail is that they don't know what else to measure. So now that I've covered that in Chapter 4:

Control Points, you can see that the things leaders should measure are never the details. So the even bigger problem with executives who focus too much on detail is that they are then not as focused on control points and outcomes as they should be.

NEVER MOVE DETAIL UP

A useful rule of thumb is that you should never move detail up in the organization: Insights move up. Detail stays down.

Every manager at each level is responsible for turning detail into useful insights and action plans—these are the things that should be moving up. That's how your organization builds value and makes progress. But some executives just won't accept that.

The more operational detail you personally process and run your staff through, the less likely you are going to scale your business. You just won't have time. You will all be reviewing so much detail that the market will move on without you, and you'll still be looking at phase review checkpoints for dozens of projects and next quarter's budget spreadsheets.

Your managers are not doing their jobs if they are bringing their level of detail up to you. You are not doing your job if you are requesting it. Everyone shouldn't need to keep tuning detailed data and presenting it to executives. They should be focused on doing the work, not creating endless reports about it. As a leader you should be finding another way to get the information you need.

DEAL WITH YOUR ADDICTION

As an executive, if you are addicted to detail, it can be scary to let go, and this requires another level of Valor. **One of the best things you can do is admit to yourself that your need for detail is for your own entertainment, not because the business needs it.**

Sure you may catch someone out or add something in the detail every now and then, but what you are really doing is competing with your managers, and by doing so you are constraining the value of your whole organization. By insisting on remaining the most expert in the detail, you are ensuring that your organization can never get any smarter than you are.

The job of a leader is to build a highly capable team that can deliver, but that can also learn and evolve and get even more capable over time, as we discussed in Chapter 11: Building Capacity. If you keep everyone reviewing detail because that makes you feel comfortable, you are missing an opportunity to develop your organization.

A much better way to deal with your addiction is to allow your managers to do their jobs; question them on strategies, control points, and outcomes (not challenge them on details); and then go right to the individuals doing the work to get your personal, psychological detail fix. At least this way you are saving the time of all the levels of managers in between. You get your details, but you don't slow business progress by involving everyone in all the detail.

When you are talking to individuals, ask questions and listen. But be careful not to overtly judge them and never assign work to them directly. If you discover something you'd like to see changed, make sure the work assignment gets passed down through the management chain. Skipping levels in conversations is fine, but skipping levels in work assignments is never okay.

Never assign work if you are not the immediate manager. As soon as you assign work out of the normal chain of hierarchy, the manager feels dis-empowered and the employee feels confused and stressed, not knowing whom they should listen to and what they should prioritize.

What About Google and Microsoft?

I often get questions about Google and Microsoft, who are legendary for having top executives who remain fully versed in huge amounts of detail.

There are two important points here. These companies are unique, vivid examples and as such are not great comparisons. But if you still want to look to them as a model, it's critical to note that an additional part of their cultures is very empowering to the individuals. Although the executives *can* handle the detail, they don't do it in a way that keeps people below them from growing.

That's the real problem. If you want to stay in the details, make sure you do it in such a way that you get out of the way! Let your teams come to their own insights and conclusions. That can't stay your job forever for everything. Don't use Google and Microsoft as an excuse to stay addicted to detail and avoid doing your higher-level job of managing control points and building capacity in your team.

Keep Control of the Outcome, But Free Yourself Up from Inspecting the Details

Many leaders fall into a mode of thinking that if they want to delegate well, and be able to step away from tracking the detail personally, that they will need to live with the risk of it all going wrong. They believe that the leadership challenge is to learn to psychologically deal with the loss of control. Nope!

The trick to delegating effectively is to do it in a way that you still feel comfortable that the right outcome is being achieved. No extra Valor is required, because the point here is to get more comfortable with what you are tracking and learning, not less!

Create systems and processes that feed you the insights and information about how the work is going that make you feel completely comfortable, without your needing to review all the details personally. Your system should have triggers that measure and report progress, and communicate problems and risks along the way. Don't learn to live with more risk; do a better job managing it—but in a fraction of the time. You need to come up with the few key measures (control points) that impact the business growth—and track those relentlessly. You'll stay comfortable and in charge. You reduce risk. You get there. And you save loads of time. See also Chapter 22: Tracking and Consequences for ideas on how to track progress in a non-detailed, highly productive way.

NEXT

You can't move forward without some conflict and disagreement because shallow agreement, while more comfortable in the moment, actually blocks action over the long term. How will you identify and manage the productive conflict necessary to move your initiative forward?

CHAPTER 20

Clarity and Conflict

Expose and Master Necessary
Conflict—Don't Avoid It

WHAT EVERYONE IS THINKING

Wow, we've been waiting for a decision on the strategy for a really long time . . . I wish the executives would finally give us the answer on this . . . I'm not sure what to work on. I'm not sure what to tell customers and partners . . . I guess I'll just continue to wait . . .

UNCERTAINTY IS EXPENSIVE

What are the unresolved strategic issues in your company? What are the decisions that never seem to get closed? Are we a product or service company? Should we do an exclusive agreement? Should we be selling through different partners? Should we upgrade our platform, or build on the one we have? Should we change our pricing for global customers or optimize regionally?

As a leader, one of your biggest responsibilities is to remove uncertainty. You need to make the big decisions. Period. Don't let them fester.

Uncertainty is a huge hidden expense and a generator of stress and low productivity in your team. It is very un-motivating to get to work and not know what you should be working on. When people are confused, there's the obvious expense of work not getting done—as uncertainty causes people to wait for decisions instead of working. But there is another damaging and expensive side of uncertainty: people doing the wrong work.

The Wrong Work

It's not strategic questions going unanswered that cause the problem. It's that they get answered every day, differently, by frontline employees who are all making different choices.

Unresolved strategic issues don't just stay in the boardroom until you finally get them answered. Every unanswered strategic question leaves legions of people in your organization deciding for themselves as they go along. Everyone is less productive and more busy than they would be with clear direction. The problem is the inconsistent outcomes that are created by everyone taking their best guess while waiting for the strategy from above.

Here is an interesting example: A company I worked with had two business units. At the executive level, it was a political war. They could not commit to a decision. Was one or the other business unit the primary mission of the company? Or should both businesses get equal attention and investment? They could not decide. This debate went on indefinitely.

So what happened? Hundreds of frontline, individual contributors had to wonder, debate, and make up their own answer to the most strategic question in the company: What business are we in?

Here is an example of how this caused the company to undermine its strategy. The lack of an answer to the core question played out at customer events. Without clear direction from above, every frontline event manager had to make a concrete decision for how to present the company at the event. They had signage for both businesses in their inventory. So they each had to decide on their own, "Do we hang one sign or both? Do we make one bigger? Put one on top? Or give them equal treatment?"

They all did their best, but of course, they all made different decisions. And different local politics ensured that the company was never represented the same way twice! Because the executives left this uncertainty, the most fundamental positioning of the company was executed differently at every single event. And this resulted in wasted time, wasted money, wasted opportunity, and failure to scale. This is such a tangible example of what can happen when there is a lack of strategic clarity. The company failed to build its brand recognition consistently in the market.

LEADERS NOTE: Be right or wrong, but never unclear.

Clarity Is the Secret Sauce for Execution

In Chapter 5: Resource Reality, I talked about the fact that your strategy is where you put your resources. And if you want to get something done, you better make sure that the right resources are assigned to it.

Creating real clarity about resources is where the biggest source of conflict starts. Once you get concrete about what you intend to do—*when? how? what? who? where does the money come from?*—you'll raise all kinds of opportunity for disagreement.

For example, if you just say, "Our goal is to sell solutions at a higher level in our customer base," everyone can feel happy, agree, and get along.

But as soon as you create clarity, you are inviting conflict: "But to do that means that we will take our top five reps, target them at these five strategic accounts, give the rest of their accounts to others, and change their comp plan. We'll divert marketing budget from the next product launch to create client specific marketing for these five accounts." That is an example of describing in a concrete way what you are actually going to do, so you can do it, but it also represents the kind of clarity that invites conflict. You need to be comfortable with exposing this type of conflict.

Many teams avoid this kind of clarity and opt for a high-level, false sense of agreement and pleasantness, instead of facing and working through the discomfort. If you never take this step of stating clearly what you are actually going to do, your strategy will stall. Everyone will just nod their heads and go back to work. Having the Valor to invite and then work through productive conflict is the only way forward.

Nodding Heads

I used to think that a roomful of nodding heads around the table was a good sign. *Nodding heads means we all agree, and we are going to go forth and do what we just talked about.* Man, was I wrong. There are all kinds of reasons why people nod their heads.

What Everyone Is Thinking

I will get out of this meeting quicker if I just nod my head. . . . I wasn't actually listening, but everyone else is nodding their head, so I will too . . . I'd actually like to raise a concern, but my opinion isn't respected, so why bother stating it? . . . I really don't agree but it will be easier to nod my head now and sabotage this decision later, behind the scenes. I'll nod my head because it won't matter anyway—we never follow through with these kinds of things.

It's generally much easier to just sit in the meeting and nod your head than it is to voice your concern or disagreement, because it avoids conflict.

EXPOSING AND RESOLVING NECESSARY CONFLICT

Here are some ideas for how to create clarity and work though necessary conflict with your team.

Clarify the Desired Outcome

First, be really clear about the desired outcome. Define what, specifically, is expected. Be really clear about:

- How the big goal breaks down clearly into smaller, concrete parts
- Who is responsible for each piece
- How each piece is resourced
- What doing something different in each case means to the old way of doing something
- How the roles of specific people change
- What the new tasks and deliverables are

- What the new behaviors and values that are expected at each level are
- How the success of each role will be measured
- What the consequences are for not doing the new thing
- What will be communicated

Don't Give People the Chance to Passively Agree

To continue the previous example, this sales organization that I worked with had a goal to sell higher up in organizations. They all agreed on that. But then to create real clarity about what they were going to *do* I asked the following:

- Do you expect every rep to spend some time on strategic deal making? How much time? Doing what, exactly?
- Will you pilot this in a few accounts with a few key sales reps? Which reps? Which accounts? What happens to the rest of their accounts?
- Will you offer the same products? Or will you need to create new product/solution offers to appeal at a higher level?
- How will you engage customers differently? Are people trained to do that? Who will be trained?
- Does this mean that you will split the team into tactical and strategic teams?
- Will you change the comp plans of the sales team?

Again, once we had this level of discussion, first there was a lot of arguing, but then they were able to come up with a plan with concrete tasks, owners, measures, and communications about it. Everyone knew what to do and what to expect each quarter over the course of the Middle.

Clarity and Creativity

Just a note: If you are at all concerned that this level of clarity eliminates creativity and innovation, quite the opposite happens. When you tell people clearly what is expected, why, and how it will be measured, it gives them goals and constraints that actually improve creativity. It's the lack of clarity, and not being sure what to work on or why it matters, that de-motivates people and gives them too vague a target to be inventive.

THE TEAM WILL NEVER MAKE TRADE-OFFS

I have never seen even the most well-intentioned teams resolve resource conflicts by moving resources from one thing to another. Teams spend hours and hours staring at the numbers, trying to decide where to cut to meet the new lower cost target or create funding for a new investment. These budgeting meetings can go on for hours, days, weeks, and months . . . It's painful. One of the reasons these meetings are painful is because the subject matter is painful, but another reason is because they don't go anywhere. You just keep talking.

And if you ask your team to go make this happen offline (so you can end this bloody meeting!), and come back and report, what each team member tends to come back with is a better prepared justification for why they need to keep all their money.

These meetings are good and necessary for you to get smarter about everything, and get everyone's input for what they think is most important. But these meetings are not good for actually making the trade-off decisions. That is your job. Have the Valor to assign top-down budgets if necessary.

Shift Resources or Die

One of the most notable examples of not dealing with resource clarity and trade-offs that I experienced was when I was working with the leadership team of a tech company. There were about 12 managers in the room, and we defined a single ruthless priority of getting a new product out into the market by the following March.

This was truly a ruthless priority, and the group was in total alignment. Everyone in the room agreed that if they did not get an initial version of this product into the market that they would die—meaning that their business would lose credibility in the market and would likely be shut down by the parent company.

Everyone agreed. They all nodded their heads.

So then I took them through the steps of creating clarity about what they will *do* and putting concrete milestones on a timeline as we discussed in Chapter 3: Timing and Momentum. It became clear that if they did not start development work on this within the next three weeks, they would never make the timeline. My part is in italics:

OK, you all agree this must be done. There is no scenario where you can not do this and remain viable. Do you have a team in place to do this work?

No.

How many people would you need?

Seventeen engineers.

Do you have the skills in your organization to fill these 17 positions or do you need to hire from the outside?

We have the skills in our organization.

Since this is so important and urgent, why not use some time in this meeting to re-assign the people now?

We can't do that.

Do all of these people report to the people who are in this room, or does this involve approval from other groups?

They all report to us.

How many engineers total report to all of you in this room?

Seven hundred.

I'm sorry, so why can't you move 17 out of 700 engineers now?

Because we'd need to involve HR; it takes time . . . *But didn't you just all agree that without putting this product in the market in March, you are all going to die? And if you don't start right now, you won't get there? It seems like you are saying that you would all prefer to run off the cliff together rather than move these 17 people.*

At this moment a very senior executive, who just happened to be auditing the meeting, came to the front of the room and said, "I have to ask the same question. Why are we not just doing this now?"

As it turned out, there was a guy sitting on the side of the room turning gray. Fifteen of the 17 engineers would be coming from his team. No one in the room had the guts to expose this conflict. The guy himself kept quiet, and everyone else did not feel it was their place to speak up.

It was fascinating to me that all of them were literally *not* going to make the move that saved the business because they did not want to hurt the feelings of one person. So instead of one person potentially losing his team, they would all lose their jobs. **For the sake of avoiding conflict, they were willing to let the whole business fail.**

As it turned out, the visiting executive took the guy whose team would need to shift out into the hall, and in a matter of moments, gave him a new charter. They both came back with smiles on their faces and within minutes the 17 people were moved.

**If you are not willing to deal with conflict,
you will not move forward!**

NEXT

Another form of conflict avoidance is decision avoidance. Decision means commitment to action, which is always scarier than continuing to wait and do more study. How will you make your team better at making critical decisions?

Read on . . .

CHAPTER 21

Decision Stall

Accelerate Effective Decision Making

WHAT EVERYONE IS THINKING

We are so slow to make decisions around here. It takes forever. And if we ever do make a decision we don't seem to ever stick to it.

With any amount of data, making a decision is hard—because a decision is a commitment to do something specific. It's much easier psychologically to just keep talking and studying because making a decision puts you at risk of being wrong. So you are never wrong if you never choose! And when you feel like you don't have enough data, committing to a decision is even scarier.

You really want to make a good decision, so you ask your team for more information so that you can personally review the situation and the progress. You schedule a business review to see the additional data and review the options again so that you can make a better decision.

WHAT EVERYONE IS THINKING

OMG, not another business review! We spend so much time researching and preparing for business reviews, we don't get to do our work! Ugh . . . we need to gather even more data and make yet another PowerPoint presentation. The execs have requested a review of the options. This needs to be the top priority for our team for the next three weeks. Delay your work because we all have to prioritize the research and the prep meetings for this review.

ARE YOU IMPLEMENTING YOUR STRATEGY OR STUDYING IT?

I was working with a CEO and his executive team on their strategy when we came to an interesting point in the day about their business needing a game-changing initiative. The group discussed several potential game changers that they had previously researched. We narrowed the list to three really cool ideas.

Then came the big question: Which is *the* one? Where will this team focus and invest to create a dramatic shift in their market? At this point in the meeting the team was feeling pretty good about the choices, but decided that the next step would be to take these ideas and study them for three more weeks and come back with a recommendation of which one to pursue.

"Why not decide right now?" I asked.

The team had entered this meeting wanting to get aligned on their strategy and come out with clear actions to implement it. Now they were going off for more study. So, I asked, "Why not pick now? What more, or what specifically can you learn in three weeks that you don't know today? How likely is it that you will learn something that will make you choose something different than you would choose today?"

The team realized that in three weeks, they probably would not learn anything materially different than what they already knew. That's the thing about being a game changer: **Leaders never have all the data. That's why they are leaders.**

Start Moving Forward

So they decided. They picked one. Instead of leaving the meeting with a bunch of tasks to study three choices, right there in the meeting we worked on the action plan to get one game changer started. We evaluated the stakeholders and adversaries, cataloged resource requirements, and created the list of the first five questions to be answered and subsequent decisions to be made. We put dates in place for the first draft of the business proposal. We talked about the concrete milestones on the timeline and brainstormed an approach for getting employee buy-in. They were moving forward.

Think about how much time this team saved. Without a decision, multiple people would have left the room with a task to study for three weeks. That would create a three-week delay in their day job *and* a three-week delay in starting work on the new strategy. Instead they chose to MOVE forward. They left with productive tasks to make actual progress.

Why Is It Hard to Decide?

When I work with groups, I find two surprising reasons why they have trouble deciding. In addition to the fear of making a bad choice or of the risk that comes with choice, one of two other very interesting things often happens:

1. **The leader does not want to force it through:** The study is seen as an opportunity to get the participation and buy-in of the team, so the leader is not seen as dictating the decision top down.

2. **The team thinks the leader requires more information:** The study is seen as an opportunity for the team to satisfy the leader that their recommendation is valid because the choices have been fully studied and justified.

You Are Allowed to Decide!

What is so interesting is that in many cases, the team actually doesn't mind if the leader states his choice, and the leader does not actually require more data! They just get locked in this default behavior to collect more data to satisfy each other's needs, which don't actually exist.

Talk about it. Make a decision. You are allowed. This is yet another time when the unstructured conversation that we talked about in Chapter 12 can save the day.

There is a time for market analysis and study, and there are times when either you know the answer, or there is no more useful data to be had. When you think you have reached this point, ask yourself these questions:

- Why am I not deciding now?
- What additional data is available that is going to help me?
- What will be materially different after more study?

By all means, if there is knowable data, go find it. But if you've exhausted the knowable data, stop studying! Start moving something forward and learn as you go.

GETTING ACTUAL FEEDBACK: THEORY VS. PRACTICE

It's important to always consider the trade-off between further study and the cost of that study. If you study something for another three months and you don't get any data that changes your decision, you have lost three months in your development schedule to implement it. And if instead, you accomplish it three months early without further study, the worst case is that you made the wrong choice.

But there is huge value in knowing for sure.

When you put something out there, you get the opportunity to get real feedback. You have a bigger advantage with an earlier delivery and real feedback than you would get by studying longer to make something theoretically more perfect. And you also have the extra time you didn't spend studying to recover in a more certain way because you bought some extra time and got actual feedback!

Study only gives you theoretical knowledge.

Putting something out in the world gives you real knowledge.

A decision always feels more risky than further study or conversation, but decision and action will always yield valuable results.

If your action turns out as you wished, you learned something real and valuable. If your action does not turn out as you wished, you learned something real and valuable—more valuable than an infinite amount of theoretical knowledge.

Fail Quickly

If you fail, fail quickly. Don't try to save a bad idea by throwing more money at it. Recognize it was a bad idea and move on. Learn, then try something else if necessary. No company does everything right. One time a mentor told me something profound about success and mistakes:

The most successful companies are the ones that can fund their mistakes.

Success comes from doing stuff. No company will ever get it all right. Success does not come from getting it right all the time. It comes from being able to recover from mistakes and keep going.

THE COST OF REQUESTS

Asking even simple questions can create a similar kind of cost and can stall your progress. It's important to be aware of this.

Here is an example: One time when I was running a large organization, I asked the financial analyst on my team, "What is the current headcount in our organization?"

He said, "How accurate an answer do you need?" I said, "What do you mean?" His response surprised me. At this point I honestly thought he would simply answer, "1,134."

But then he said, "If you want a number within 10 percent, I could let you know by the end of the day, but if you want a more accurate number, it will probably take me a couple of weeks to check all the systems, and get inputs from my counterparts around the world, and then check with HR about exits and pending offers . . ."

That was a big eye opener for me:

1. Thank God he asked! I never would have intended to have him work on this for two weeks and involve loads of other people. I was mostly just curious.
2. I realized that when an executive asks a question, the multiplier effect on the work done throughout the organization can be a very expensive thing.

If You Are the Recipient of Executive Requests

Really know that not all executive requests are created equal. Sometimes it's a big deal with the world watching, and sometimes it's just a casual request or curiosity. Organizations have a tendency to accept all executive requests as urgent and vitally important. They are not!

Never just start working on something. **The first thing you should do when given a task is to start thinking, not start working.**

Pause. Think: How much does this matter, really? You need to clarify. The more you clarify, the less work you will need to do. And the less rework you will need to do later.

Here are some straightforward clarifying questions you can ask an executive to find out how much work you should really be doing on the request:

So I can do the best possible job for you . . .

1. Can you help me understand what this will be used for? Is this just for you? Or do you need this because someone else is asking? Do you know why they are asking and what they need it for? What do you need to make happen with this after you get this from me? Is the way we did this last time useful for you? Or should we think about a better way to accomplish the outcome?

2. How much time and cost do you want this effort to take? Is this worth a big investment of time? Is this worth moving resources from something else? Or should I be looking for a way to do this as minimally and efficiently as possible?

If You Are the Executive Making Requests

Whenever you are making a request, you should always be thinking of the cost of getting your outcome. Know that even asking what seems to be a simple question can send dozens of people running around for weeks. So each time you make a request, also share the relative importance of the request to other work and give it a budget: "Get me whatever you can accomplish in two hours," or "Drop everything for the next week until this is done."

Don't make the person guess. And don't let your request inadvertently stop them from doing something that is actually more important unless you are sure it is really worth it.

Consensus vs. Command

Another decision blocking behavior I see is too much emphasis on consensus. Throughout my whole career I kept hearing discussions about consensus vs. command, and those discussions always rubbed me the wrong way.

What actually works was never such a mystery to me. The problem is that people would talk about consensus or command as the only two choices for management style. "Nice" organizations who moved too slowly were dismissed as "consensus-driven," and nasty, aggressive organizations that bullied people and got results by leaving a trail of casualties had leaders who were seen as "commanding." What works is simply this:

1. Listen to everyone to get the most robust and complete input.
2. Then allow the decision maker to make the decision.
3. Move forward.

The Problem with "Consensus"

Consensus breaks down when the discussion never moves past the input and discussion phase. It breaks down because leaders wait for everyone to agree before moving forward. Everyone will never agree. You get stuck. Or you go so slow you become irrelevant.

The Problem with "Command"

Command breaks down when you make a clear, fast decision and just give orders without letting anyone speak their mind and share their opinions and knowledge. When you seek no input, people are not bought in, they don't know what to do next, and they don't feel respected. So they are not motivated to move forward.

The Way to Move Forward: Get Input, Make a Decision

If you have time to get input, you are always better off to have the discussion, encourage the debate—and then make a decision. I once had a new staff that was used to the consensus-oriented, "don't-act-until-everyone-agrees-which-is-basically-never" school of management. I remember, after a heated discussion, the first time I pointed to the person on my team who owned the decision and said, "Okay, you've heard all of our input, it's your decision, what do you decide?"

Everyone was stunned. "Can we really *do* that?" They couldn't believe that we were allowed to stop talking and move forward. They were not sure that I was allowed to do that! I assured them that I was. It's the technique I have always used. And once this team got used to it, they appreciated the opportunity to move forward.

The key to moving forward:

- Don't let the bad rap on "consensus" management prevent you from getting input.
- And don't let the bad rap on "command" prevent you from making a decision once you have the input.

DEBATE VS. GO

A great, simple tool I use to encourage this input-then-decision style of management is the model of "debate" phase vs. "go" phase. For every initiative or decision, there is debate time and there is go time.

Debate Time

During debate time, I make it clear that I want to hear people's opinions. I want to hear the arguments. I want everyone to fight for their point of view. That's how I get the best and most complete information. Then after debate time is over, I make it clear who owns the decision, and make sure the decision gets made.

Go Time

Then I make it clear that we are in go time. The decision is communicated and the action is officially kicked off. This is the time to engage in the work, not in the debate. The debate phase is over.

Expectations and Trust

This simple frame and set of labels builds an atmosphere of higher trust because people can understand the rules of the game. By setting this structure, you can make it clear that during debate time, the expected and valued behavior is to speak up. Then once you announce the decision has been made and make it clear that it's go time, people trust that you will stick to the decision, and that the expected and valued behavior is action, not more talking.

NEXT

Something always goes wrong. Something will always be late. How will you keep momentum and make forward progress when there are setbacks?

Read on . . .

CHAPTER 22

Tracking and Consequences

How to Identify and Recover from Setbacks

WHAT EVERYONE IS THINKING

We don't seem to follow through on things around here. We talk about important stuff we need to do, but if we miss a deadline nothing really happens. I don't think we are very good at execution.

You cannot execute a transformation throughout the long Middle without something going wrong along the way. As a leader, you need a strategy for addressing the problems and gaps, and getting the program moving forward again.

WHEN NOTHING HAPPENS

Many executives ask for my help by saying, "My team isn't good at executing." So I get to observe execution issues at many different types of companies.

One of the things that many companies seem to miss is the connection between execution and consequences. The reason why many organizations have so much trouble making strategic progress and doing what they intend to do, on time, is because when they fail to meet a deadline . . . nothing happens.

The date comes and goes and no one talks about it.

People who were on the hook either assume that they have been granted more time, or it wasn't that important to begin with. And then there is no new focused deadline established because no one is talking about it at all.

If you don't address the very first deadline slip on the strategic thing, the urgent tactical demands of the moment take over, and strategic progress becomes a low priority and a distant memory. People will say, "Aha, I guess we are *not* still doing this."

If you need to make strategic progress, you can't let any deadline come and go and leave the failure totally unacknowledged and unexamined.

Not addressing a miss sends all the wrong messages and sets a very low standard of execution.

What you are communicating (by not communicating) is:

- It really wasn't that important after all.
- It doesn't really matter that it didn't get done.
- There are no consequences around here for missing a deadline.
- We're not serious about meeting our commitments.
- Late is okay.

Motivation Requires Consequences

Every time you avoid addressing an issue with someone who is not delivering or missing a schedule, you destroy some trust, especially with your high performers. In addition to degrading trust, an environment with no consequences offers no motivation or reward for performing well. People think: *Why bother? Nothing happens if you don't deliver on time, so why knock yourself out?*

Lack of consequences is actually de-motivating because people need their work to matter, as we talked about in Chapter 15: Getting People to Actually Care. A good leader will use every tool in the box to get people to personally care.

Without measures and consequences, anything else you do for motivation becomes hollow and point- less. The work has to matter. If failing to get it

done on time doesn't matter, by definition, the work doesn't matter.

ENFORCING CONSEQUENCES

What Do You Say?

Many managers get uncomfortable with enforcing consequences because they don't know what the appropriate "punishment" should be. When someone does something wrong, what do you do? Do you fire someone for missing a deadline? Do you fire someone for being late to a meeting?

Have the Valor to Have the Difficult Conversation

You don't need to fire people every time something goes wrong. But you do need to address it. Don't just accept this behavior. I see leaders think, *Well this isn't enough of a problem to fire the person . . .* , but because they are not comfortable having a difficult conversation, they do nothing.

You don't need to fire the person, but you do need to confront the poor behavior. Acknowledge it. Have the conversation. There are so many options between termination and nothing! You don't need to be a tyrant. But you do need to have a conversation. No matter how small a deadline seems, if it is missed, it should be addressed. Here is a script for the conversation:

This is unacceptable. You did not deliver. What happened? Do you realize the downstream problems this causes? What is your proposal to recover? How do you propose we now get this finished and *address the customer/sales/market issue this has created? How will you ensure this does not happen again?*

Even if the end result seems the same, that the new date has still slipped two weeks out, the fact that you had the conversation will resonate far beyond this one deadline.

If you always have the conversation, it will help your organization see and feel that you are serious about execution, and that schedules and commitments really do matter. If you always ask, "What happened? How to do you intend to recover?" the act of having this conversation sends the message that it is *not okay* to miss a deadline.

And then the next time people will think, *If I miss a deadline, something uncomfortable is going to happen.*

Sure, it can be uncomfortable to have a conversation about missed goals and consequences, but if you miss a goal, it should be uncomfortable! That's the point.

You missed a deadline. That should not be pleasant, comfortable news for anyone. It's not about coming down extra hard on someone or being disrespectful or nasty. It's about moving the business forward. Also, I find that strong performers take a lot of ownership in these conversations and put even more pain on themselves than they get from you. And, in general, people will start self-managing, and delivering on time, to avoid those conversations. Everyone needs to have the Valor to own it and address it when a goal is missed.

Will You Become a Tyrant?

I have had kind managers who were tough with consequences, and I have had managers who were bullies. These are completely different things. You do not need to worry about becoming a bad person by calling out poor performance. As long as you put the business outcome as the motivation for the conversation, you are not attacking the person as a bully would. As long as you can ask yourself, "Is this conversation moving the business forward?" you are on the high ground.

You can be kind to people and tough on results.

Avoiding the conversation does not move the business forward.

Having the conversation does move the business forward.

A good leader will realize that addressing missed deadlines and failures will create an organization that:

1.   Builds trust, especially with high performers
2.   Can learn from its mistakes

3. Will deliver on time, more predictably
4. Develops higher performing individuals
5. Creates products and services that hit market needs better and sooner

This form of productive persistence is what lets your organization know you are serious, and that what they are doing really matters. When an organization is having trouble executing, I often find that underneath it is a lack of the sort of Valor that is required to enforce consequences.

DEVELOP BETTER HABITS ON SMALL THINGS

As a leader, you have a personal responsibility to set a high standard of execution.

I have found that small habits are a big indicator of big habits. If you have poor execution on the small things, like being on time for meetings, you are likely to also have poor execution on big things like product delivery schedules.

This idea was described really well in Malcolm Gladwell's book, *The Tipping Point* (Back Bay Books, 2002). I'll paraphrase a lot here to get quickly to my point, but I recommend reading this directly in *The Tipping Point* if you are interested.

Malcolm Gladwell talked about how serious crime in New York City was greatly reduced in the 1980's, not by directly going after the big crimes, but by making a concerted effort to eliminate two small crimes: first, jumping the turnstiles to avoid paying subway fare; and, second, graffiti on the subways.

Police started relentlessly arresting people for turnstile jumping, and every single night, any train car with graffiti on it got pulled off the tracks and painted over.

The point is this: People with intentions to commit bigger crimes saw this enforcement of these minor things and thought, *If they are that serious about these small offenses, they must be really serious about bigger ones. This is not an environment where crime is tolerated.*

It worked.

Late to Meetings

Being late to meetings may not seem like a big deal; in fact, most organizations laugh it off: "Yeah, we're really bad about that around here." But tolerating chronic lateness and just accepting it as an amusing part of the culture is sending a subtle but strong message: *Commitments don't matter here.* So you are undermining your ability to achieve your long-term goals.

> **When everyone is chronically late to meetings and you don't address it, you are sending a cultural signal: we are not serious about what we say we are going to do.**

If, instead, you set and enforce an expectation that meetings will start and end on time, and then do it—not only do you get the huge benefit of cost and time savings from more productive meetings, you get the additional, even-bigger benefit of an expectation in your organization that it matters what we say and commit to. You get a higher performing culture that more naturally embraces commitments and deadlines. *If we are this serious about managing meetings, we are also serious about managing our schedules, commitments, and business.*

One of the fascinating things is that this is so very easy to turn around. You don't have to fire someone for being late to a meeting to change the culture; you just have to say something. When the person walks in late you simply say:

> What part of "this meeting starts at 8 am" did you not understand? This meeting starts at 8 am, and I expect you to be here at 8 am. It's 8:04. What makes you think it's okay for you to come at 8:04?

Believe me, you only need to say this one or maybe two times. Everyone in the room will be cringing, and no one in the room will want to hear it again. Your meetings will start on time.

(You need to be on time too.) Leaders who want their teams to deliver on time, but who don't show up on time for their own meetings, frankly drive me crazy. By not showing up on time, yet demanding excellent execution, they are sending a mixed message about the importance of commitments and the standards of execution they personally find acceptable.

THE GAP BETWEEN COMMITTED AND DONE
How I Narrowly Escaped Disaster

When I got my first big job, managing a group of about 200 people with multiple layers of management beneath me, I did not have experience getting things done leading an organization of this size. This was the software development job to implement the SEI process and improve quality I talked about in Chapter 17: Burn the Ships at the Beach.

The Gap Between Assigning and Doing

I am really good at translating high-level strategy into super-clear actions with owners and measures. I see the big picture, I see the opportunity for how to win, I see what is in the way, and I can prioritize the right concrete tasks that will ensure we make strategic progress. So with my staff, we quickly got to the point where we had a strategy and we had owners and tasks agreed. Everyone was clear about what we needed to do and why. And we had a schedule with control point measures and deadlines. Commence head nodding.

But then . . .

Everyone left the room and went back to work. Because the assignments were so clear and committed and resourced, I assumed the new work was being worked on. What I didn't know was that there was a whole other body of work to be done to ensure that everyone actually did those tasks. There was tracking and pestering and reporting and review necessary. Not only did I not know that this had to be done, this was not a type of work I was personally good at. And I was too busy doing other work to be able to do a good job at this part, even if I could have.

This is where my hero, the process manager Scott Jordan who was on my staff, saved the day. This was a true gift. I did not know what a process manager did. I did not know that I needed a process manager. I did not personally hire Scott. But even though I didn't know it, or appreciate it at the beginning, I had someone on my team who was brilliant at tracking execution progress and did it without my direction—thank God! Here's what he did:

- **Capture:** He would sit in those staff meetings and take all the notes about what was decided and committed and he would write it up, distribute it, *and* turn it into a project plan with dependencies and timelines.
- **Daily Follow-Up:** Then he would go around to every task owner, every week, and say, "How are you doing on this?" He would exert regular, personal visibility and pressure on what was committed.
- **Reporting:** Then he would create a report and bring it into our staff meeting every week and let us know what was getting done on schedule and what (and who) was slipping.

With that steady effort, he enabled us to make sure we all got done what we committed to. He made it easy for me to have the discussion and enforce consequences for being late, because what was supposed to happen was spelled out so very clearly.

This was invaluable. Without this process, we would have failed to get stuff done on time. There is no question in my mind about this.

I really can't emphasize this enough. As the leader, I was feeling pretty good about my strategic thinking and my ability to translate the high-level goals into specific, concrete actions to get there. But as the leader, I was also too busy with strategy, financial planning, communications, customers, traveling to multiple sites, and general corporate stuff to be the one to personally go around and get updates from everyone, and create reports to track it all.

I can say without a doubt, without my process manager, I would have failed.

My good luck to have Scott on my team, who knew what to do before I knew it, was for certain a turning point in my career. If I would have failed to deliver, I would have failed in my job. I would have failed to advance.

I always describe myself as a leader who builds teams that can execute. While that is true, I would not have turned into that type of leader without Scott, and I would not have known to recruit someone like him, who had the natural strengths, skills, and energy to do this type of work. I have recruited someone to play this role on my team forever after.

I also want to mention here that Scott's work kept us all out of the details. He turned all the details into insights that we could review in a productive manner. Our control points were described in the form of phases. If we cleared the phase, that meant a zillion things went right, but we did not all spend time reviewing all the details. Scott created the framework that turned details into insights like I discussed in Chapter 19: Detail.

HIRE YOUR HERO

If you do not have the time, strengths, skills, or motivation to do the tracking and follow-through piece, the important thing to take away here is that you need to have this ability in your organization. Hire this person. This is not a low-level administrative job. Have this person report directly to you and give them a lot of power. The person in this role needs to be someone who understands the business and someone who can understand the pressure you are under personally. They need to be able to enforce priorities when you are running out of time and you are not there.

It needs to be someone who can influence the people on your team who need to do the work, to do the work. Don't put on-time execution at risk. It's too important. Get help to track and measure execution.

Hard, Boring, and Required (But Worth It)

A big part of managing execution is paying attention to deadlines and doing something about it when they are not met.

A mentor of mine describes this as "doing the hard, boring, and required." Once again, it requires Valor to keep doing hard, boring, and required stuff throughout the long Middle.

Perhaps this is not the most fun and exciting part of your leadership job—keeping track of commitments and following through when things go wrong. But I have found that it actually doesn't take a lot of "enforcement" to create better habits and move the culture in the right direction. You need to always address the things that have established commitments. If you tolerate chronic poor performance on small things, it's much harder to achieve good performance on big things.

NEXT

You can lead a transformation from the top, but you can't *do* a transformation from the top. You need Everyone. How will you get enough of the people in your organization doing the new things that the business needs?

Read on . . .

PART 4

E = Everyone

You Can Lead a Transformation from the Top, but You Can't Do a Transformation from the Top

Although you need Valor, your Valor alone cannot keep a whole organization moving forward through the Middle. You need everyone to move forward.

You need to create an atmosphere of trust and motivation. You need to foster rich conversation among *Everyone* and make the work environment look and feel different, so it reflects the changes and the new strategy. You need to make sure that Everyone can see and feel the transformation every day. You'll know that your initiative will stick when you notice that you are not the only one talking about it!

CHAPTER 23

Conversation

Change How You Communicate to Make Your Strategy Stick

Throughout this book so far, I've been talking about the fact that transformation cannot happen as a top-down process created and driven by executive effort alone. You need active involvement from everyone. And at last we are at the section of the model that is about E = Everyone.

To start on this idea, let's go back for a moment to where we began in Chapter 1: The Beginning of the Middle.

Imagine that you are in the first moments of your transformation. You have completed your planning. You have developed your strategy. You have created a presentation to communicate it. You're finally ready to roll it out. So now you hold an all-hands meeting, you take the stage, and you begin to communicate.

WHAT EVERYONE IS THINKING

Here we go again, the strategy du jour. What's it going to be this time? Hmmm . . . I just thought of a new idea to solve a problem I was working on; I wish I wasn't in this meeting so I could keep working on it . . . What was on my Costco shopping list? Oops, I forgot to tell my son that his karate lesson was canceled . . .

In other words, people are thinking about whatever they are thinking about! They are not thinking about your new strategy.

You need to remember that you have been thinking about your new strategy for a long time. You have studied it, and maybe even tested options. You have all the history and the context. You have had the motivation to make this change for a long time. You have had the time to fully internalize it, and you are ready to go forward.

But for everyone else: *They are hearing it for the first time. And they are not really listening.* They have no context. They have no history. They have no motivation to change. People hate change. Change means new stuff to do. They already feel too busy. They fear this new thing will mean even more work, or that their job will somehow get worse. They might be thinking, *I've been paying my mortgage and supporting my family for 20 years with this thing that you are now changing.* Even if these doomed thoughts are not true, as soon as they hear change is coming, people are inclined to shut down.

Also, they will have a tendency to think that you are not serious, because they have heard about many new strategies and initiatives in the past, and nothing ever happened. So why should they bother investing in this one? It won't matter anyway.

So once you deliver your presentation, although you can give yourself credit for creating a strategy, creating a presentation, and delivering a presentation, you cannot take credit for actually communicating your strategy.

TELLING DOES NOT EQUAL COMMUNICATING

Your broadcast has almost nothing to do with whether or not something has been communicated. Simply telling people your strategy does not mean they heard it.

You should never assume that just because you have told everyone your strategy (for the first time!), they were listening carefully and they internalized it—that they know what they need to do personally to act on it and how to optimize it with regard to their current work, and that they will actively do the right things to implement their piece of it.

In fact, it's kind of funny when an executive realizes that people "aren't getting it." Typically I find there is an inverse relationship between the level of emphasis an executive will use to say, "But I was very clear," and how much has actually been internalized by their audience!

CONVERSATION VS. COMMUNICATION

The right measure is never about how clearly you think you have communicated. The only right measure is about how much your audience has internalized.

You need to be ready to consider this first telling of your strategy as pretty much a throwaway effort. Yes, it's a step in the process. Yes, you need to communicate top down. But to genuinely communicate, and to get your message internalized, and for your transformation to take hold, you need to create a fundamental shift in the way that you think about communication. You need to change your existing idea of communication to instead become *conversation*—that involves everyone.

So here is the right measure of the effectiveness of your communication:

You have communicated successfully when the people in your organization are talking about it amongst themselves.

Conversation, the Control Point for Communication

Remember in Chapter 5 how we described control points as measuring the desired outcome that you want to achieve? If you use a measure of "the strategy has been communicated to everyone," that is a bad measure because it is a measure of an activity, not an outcome—so it's not a control point. Control points are called "control points" because if you can achieve the control point measure, you have achieved the desired outcome, and you can be assured that a bunch of the right things happened to deliver that outcome.

So, why not instead use the following as your control point for measuring the effectiveness of your communication: *The communication can be declared as successful only when the audience is talking about it amongst themselves.*

It's a good control point because if you see that outcome happening, that means that your audience has internalized your message well enough to talk about it, they are engaged enough to talk about it, and they are spending time and energy focused on it. It works as a control point because many good things are happening, and you don't need to measure them all individually.

For your transformation to work, the change must be part of the social fabric of the whole organization in a very real way—and that happens through conversation.

For example, when you can approach an employee at any level at random and ask, "What is the most important thing for us to be doing right now, and why?" and get the same answer most of the time, then you can say that your communication has been successful.

When I led the strategic transformation in the HP OpenView software business, I knew it was working when six months in a customer described our new strategy to an editor, and it was quoted accurately in the press, and a sales engineer in a remote part of Europe presented the strategy to a visiting colleague of mine who relayed it back to me.

Success: The conversation about my strategy was happening whether or not I was there. People in the business (and customers!) were thinking and communicating about the new strategy. We had created the right conversation, and people at all levels across the world were talking about it.

CONVERSATION CREATES FORWARD MOMENTUM AND SAFETY

It's always fascinating to me how quickly people can lose confidence that they should be doing the new thing. ("Are we still doing this?") The gravitational pull of going back to the old way is really strong because it feels more familiar and safer. Especially if you feel like you are out on a limb as the only one trying to do the new thing. Conversation is what makes people feel safe: *I am not putting myself at risk if I do the new thing. Because of this ongoing conversation about it, I know that we are all doing it.*

Here is a great example: One time I did some work for a marketing agency who decided that they wanted to do more executive-level outreach. Every client-facing person committed to spending 30 minutes per day making calls to C-level people. For the first couple of days everything went great.

Then on the third day, there was a media crisis, and one of the people jumped on that. The others saw her switch back to working on the current business and not doing her 30 minutes of new executive outreach. The next day, another couple of people stopped doing their 30 minutes of the new executive outreach to catch up on existing work. Then the rest of the others who were still doing the new executive outreach noticed now three people not doing the new thing.

Without a word of a change being spoken by anyone, the people still doing their 30 minutes per day thought, *Oh, I guess we're not doing this any more*, and they stopped. By the fifth day, no one was doing the new thing.

It's really hard to keep your organization focused on doing something new through the Middle. If there is the slightest bump in the road, they will lose confidence in the new thing and go back to their old way of working. As the leader, you need to find a way to keep the conversation going. **It's the conversation that is the visible thing that people see and experience, and that informs them, "Yes, we are still doing this!"**

What this team decided they needed to stay on track was daily conversation about the new thing. So they created a process that at 3 pm every day, someone (on a rotating schedule) would ask, "How did we all do on our C-level client outreach today?" They could share what worked and didn't work, but most importantly, they were keeping the conversation alive. It was something they could all feel and experience every single day. And with each day that went by, the new behavior became more normal, because the conversation reinforced the confidence that, "Yes, we're still supposed to be doing this."

You do not have a chance at driving lasting change until the people doing the work are talking about it on their own. Communication is still important from the top down, but it's so much more effective when it is done in such a way that it then spreads in all directions, naturally.

CONVERSATION DRIVES ACTION

Here is another excellent example of how a transformation happens by not merely communicating your intention from the top down, but by creating an opportunity for real conversation to happen throughout your organization. Conversation that creates action happens when you enable the people whom you need to implement the transformation to start talking about the transformation among themselves in an ongoing manner.

> **Ongoing conversation about change is what drives actual change and makes it stick.**

Example: Utopia Village Transforming Customer Service

Recently I had the opportunity to visit a resort on the island of Utila in Honduras called Utopia Village (www.UtopiaVillage.com). This is a beautiful place with a world-class level of service that I have not experienced in this part of the world before. It was so remarkable that I decided to talk to the owners about how they accomplished it.

The owners, Paul and Chrisna, are strongly community minded, and in an effort to support and develop the local community, they try to employ only local people at their resort instead of recruiting service-experienced staff from five-star resorts from other places in the world.

So the business transformation challenge was this: How do we educate and inspire local people who have never been outside Honduras, who have never stayed in high-end resorts or hotels, with little or no service experience at all, to deliver a world-class level of customer service?

They told me that that they focused on and emphasized just four simple rules for how to treat guests. They communicated these (initially top down) often and frequently.

1. We try to always say *yes* (be flexible, find a way to make it happen).
2. We pay attention to the *details* (notice what people like and don't like and modify the service for each person accordingly).
3. We try to *exceed* expectations (anticipate, do things without being asked, think of special things).
4. We are always there to greet guests (no guest ever leaves the resort or arrives back on the resort without a staff member being there to greet them).

Paul and Chrisna:

In the beginning the staff didn't fully understand what really was being asked of them, or in some cases why it was important or why it mattered.

They never openly resisted it. In the beginning they would nod their heads and say they understood what was expected when we discussed the rules. But in practice we just did not see the follow-through on the execution side. In the beginning we had to re-emphasize the rules many times, and we had to constantly give *lots* of examples and feedback. Eventually they started to do the small things we were asking more consistently—enough that guests started noticing.

Then, the staff started to experience the *conversation*.

The staff started to see guest comments on TripAdvisor and the guest survey forms, as well as receive direct feedback from guests. They were proud when guests noticed and said something!

By now our #1 Trip Advisor rating was a great source of pride for them. They love it when guests comment on the "exceptional service." Once this conversation was happening, we began to see them really try (without being told anymore by us) to DELIGHT guests and surprise them with small things, wonderful things that even surprised us!

To take advantage of this initial momentum the owners created another new opportunity for conversation among the staff. Using the online messaging platform WhatsApp, they created a WhatsApp Group that the staff could own called Utopia Stars. It includes every member of the staff.

Paul and Chrisna continued:

Whenever someone sees something special or fun (e.g., a colleague doing something great, a team working hard, staff waiting for the guests to arrive back on site . . .), another staff member posts a message on WhatsApp that everyone can see.

This Chat Group had an amazing impact—much more than we ever could have dreamed when it was created. Everyone follows it. Everyone can post in it. Because it is typically a photo with some basic emojis (smiley face, thumbs up, hands clapping, etc.), it breaks down all barriers. Even if you don't speak English or Spanish, the pictures and the emojis tell the story. It has created a wonderful sense of community. It also helps make people feel connected. It was a channel our young staff was familiar and comfortable with. It breaks down barriers while building a sense of community and "being part of something bigger." And it is fun.

This moved the critical conversation that motivated the right actions exactly to where it needed to be—to the staff themselves, in an application they already used to communicate.

An important part about creating conversation among the people doing the work is that you need to create the conversation where the communication of your group is already happening. If they had to employ a new communication mechanism, for example, fill out a physical form or send an email, it would not have taken hold in such a strong way. You need to be willing to initiate and join the conversation on their terms, where they are naturally active and feel comfortable, not where you feel comfortable (on email, in your office, through scrubbed employee communication memos, etc.).

This really worked! Not only is the service truly excellent and virtually flawless, the people who care most about delivering this service are the staff themselves.

Paul and Chrisna:

> When we hire new people now, we still share with them our values and the four things, but what they have learned is that the current staff shares it on their own and tells the new staff members about it. We now have minimal effort (nothing like initially) to educate and convince the new staff of what is expected and why it is important. The current staff members are the advocates and bring the new staff on board.

Now that is a successful transformation! Not only is the staff not asking "Are we still doing this?" they are the ones sharing the strategy with new staff.

It is an excellent example of moving the conversation necessary to drive the change into the right place in the organization. The conversation has taken a strong hold among the people doing the work. That's always your goal.

YOUR CONVERSATION

Remember, the Middle is a long time. How will you keep the conversation going throughout the whole Middle about what you need to happen? People need to have confidence that the new thing is the right thing to do. They need to feel safe.

The best way to make people feel safe and to motivate them to move forward is to make sure they see that all their peers are also doing it. This will happen only if their peers are talking about it.

You don't want to have to be in a position to tell people what to do every day. You want them making the right choices and decisions on their own, without your constant involvement. You want them to have the confidence that they are doing the right thing by doing the new work and supporting the strategy.

If you want something to happen, make sure everyone keeps talking about it.

Next

Conversation is the first critical step in engaging everyone. But there is even more you can do to build confidence and make your strategy truly take hold in the community. How will you make your change highly visible so that it's easy for everyone to see on any given day that, "Yes, we are still doing this"?

Read on . . .

CHAPTER 24

Decorate the Change

"Yes, We Are Really Doing This"

WHAT EVERYONE IS THINKING

We talked about a new strategy a few weeks ago, but I'm not really sure what's different. I thought I was supposed to start this new work, but now I'm getting a bit nervous that I'm the only one doing it. Maybe we changed our mind and no one told me. I am going to hang back and wait to make sure we are still doing this.

As we talked about in the last chapter, ongoing conversation among the people doing the work is a fundamental and necessary ingredient to continue to make forward progress in your transformation. But the most effective organizations take it a step further and intentionally create rituals, artifacts, and even modifications to their physical workspace to make the change highly visible throughout the whole Middle. I refer to this as "decorating the change."

A STORY ABOUT A GOAT

I'll share a story that I love about the non-profit organization, Heifer International. They have been doing their work for over 60 years.

Heifer deals primarily in livestock. They set out to transform communities (a strategic initiative) in the poorest parts of the world. They provide the livestock, along with training and breeding programs, to communities. When a family gets a goat or a heifer, or another type of animal, they are able to produce food for their family to eat, as well as produce food to sell. They become able to earn a living. When multiple families in a community are eating well and earning a living, the community is fundamentally transformed.

This is an organization for which successful, strategic transformation in a community is a matter of life or death.

"Passing On the Gift"

A key part of their community transformation success is a concept they call "passing on the gift." When a family's animal has an offspring, they are asked to give the offspring to another family in the community. Heifer has created a mechanism and a social expectation around this. It is a "passing on the gift ceremony." This is basically a party. The ceremony is, well, a ceremony. There are rituals and expectations. The animal to be passed to the new family is decorated as a special gift with ribbons and colors and flowers. The whole community participates in this ceremony when the gift is made to another family.

I was talking to an executive from Heifer, and she told me a story about some people from Heifer recently traveling in Cambodia. They saw a man on the side of the road carrying a goat that was decorated with flowers. They stopped to talk to him and asked, "What's the deal with the goat?"

He told them, "I got this goat for my family in a 'passing on the gift' ceremony." He was very happy and honored and filled with hope for the future.

The punchline: Heifer had not worked in this community for 17 years. Seventeen years!!

Talk about a strategic transformation that worked! The exact thing that they set out to do was still going, thriving, and functioning 17 years later—with no involvement from "management" whatsoever.

DECORATING THE CHANGE

That story has become my barometer for making strategic change successful. Ever since I heard it I use this story as the bar to measure how well a strategic initiative is doing: If the management walked away, how likely would it be that the initiative keeps going as intended?

How is it that this transformation stuck for so many years? And what can we learn from it?

First of all, when there was an offspring, it was not simply passed from one family to another behind the scenes. There was a ceremony that involved the *entire community*—every time. They decorated the change with the celebration, and by decorating the animal itself. Moreover, the community-wide celebration created a conversation among the entire community. To have a ceremony each and every time there was an offspring ensured that the conversation throughout the whole community continued on a regular and ongoing basis.

The transformation was kept alive because every- one could see the decoration, and everyone was part of the conversation.

DECORATE THE CHANGE THROUGH THE MIDDLE

It's important to think about how you will decorate your change.

After you communicate your strategy, you then need to create a conversation (the conversation is a primary decoration in itself), and then find other ways to decorate your change so that people can notice it in their environment and want to join in—like the story about the goat and the passing on the gift ceremony.

If someone visited your office before you started your transformation and then again in the Middle of it, what would they see? What are your decorations? What are you doing consistently to show everyone that your transformation is still important?

The following are some ideas.

Ritual

"I understood the strategy, and all I got was this lousy T-shirt."

Don't skip the T-shirt or the water bottle or the laminated ID card! Pick a couple of people within the organization to select a fun or interesting artifact that your culture will like, and use it to "decorate" the change. Asking people within the organization to do this is a good start at making conversation happen in the right place instead of making it a chore for HR and marketing departments. It is also some insurance against the result being seen as a lame offer from management. When people walk around and see that these things are all over the place, it demonstrates clearly that . . . "yes, we are really still doing this."

An amusing example of decorating the change and having the conversation be in the right place is when I had given an engineering organization an aggressive goal, and one of the engineers said, "If we make this date, I think Patty should have to wear pastel colors to work." (I have always gone for a simple, chic, black and white approach.) Well, this idea quickly took on a life of its own and resulted in the HR manager taking me to buy the frilliest and most hideous pastel pink dress imaginable, and then hanging it in my office. Then, much to my surprise, the engineers started accessorizing! My office filled up with flowered hats, pink shoes, lace gloves . . . This conversation and "decoration" stayed active among the engineers throughout the entire Middle . . . and they achieved the date. And I wore the dress. I could not have come up with a better idea! The best ideas for decorating the change are the organic ones that come from the community itself.

A Contest

A contest can be a great source of conversation and engagement among the team. Here's an excellent example.

Montana Meth, Paint the State!   One of my favorite examples of a transformation that did a remarkable job of decorating the change using a contest was the Montana Meth Project. The Montana Meth Project is a large-scale prevention program aimed at reducing first-time, teen meth use through public service messaging, public policy, and community outreach.

When they launched this program many years ago, they came up with an idea to have an art competition across the state. They called it "Paint the State." The contest was open to anyone 12 years old and over, and it had a few rules:

- The art that is created must carry one or more of the key messages of the campaign.
- The art must be visible to the public.

Many counties in the state of Montana saw participation. Then they had a contest and gave cash awards to the winners in several categories in several counties.

Think about this in terms of decorating the change:

1. The target audience becomes personally involved with the message.
2. The target audience not only discusses the message among themselves but spends time creating art that carries the message.
3. The art itself is a physical decoration. It is visible to everyone throughout the state. People see it on a daily basis.
4. The art has credibility with the target audience because it was created by the target audience.
5. The target audience is compelled to participate because there is a valuable prize.

This program got right to the heart of their target audience and brought them into the conversation by making one of the contest rules that the art had to carry the messaging of the program (conversation in the right place, brilliant!), and they decorated the change by requiring that the art had to be publicly visible (decoration visible everywhere, even more brilliant!).

They created a powerful and visible conversation among their target audience.

I've seen companies accomplish a similar kind of engagement by sponsoring contests for employees to create videos about their strategies or transformations. One company I remember created a set of games they called the "Hallway Olympics."

At the end there are a few prizes for the winners, but during the process a whole lot of people were motivated to get involved with the new strategy. These types of contests and games create a lot of conversation and a lot of decoration. All of that helps your strategy stick.

Blogs

For any strategy, initiative, or big idea that you want everyone to understand, another great way to decorate the change is to get someone blogging internally about it. Pick someone who has the interest and the knack for it. Then don't overload or overwork the process. Make sure they know it's not about perfect writing—it's about sharing the most important ideas and decisions.

The updates can just be bullets. Nothing fancy is necessary; it just needs to exist. You will find interested parties commenting and discussions happening in a very organic way. This is a big win. If I were in a corporate role now, I would insist that every project leader keep an informal blog, and I would measure them on creating conversation. This to me is a control point with an outcome: The people doing the work are conversing regularly on the blog. So many of the right things will happen if your key program leaders are sharing information in this way. I talk more about this in Chapter 27. Sharing Information.

Brown Bags, Informal Gatherings

Be on the lookout for bright spots in the organization where the organization is doing the right thing. Transformation does not take hold equally at the same time everywhere. But if you are watching, you will find those early examples of traction. When you find a bright spot, amplify it and market it! Ask that person or team to host a brown bag lunch and share how they did it. Recognize the effort. Celebrate and honor the brave people who are the first ones to implement the change. And as we talked about in Chapter 17: Burn the Ships at the Beach, protect those people and their efforts on the new work with your life, and then make them famous.

Celebrate the Program Success

Don't let real progress and finished milestones pass uncelebrated—even if it's ringing a bell (or the technology equivalent) that everyone can hear when the right kind of deal closes, or the next group implements the new system successfully. Find a way to let people know that they are achieving small victories along the way.

Decorate those moments of progress.

And don't forget to celebrate the big victories too. Work can feel really thankless for the people doing the work. Don't miss opportunities to show appreciation for the people and teams who are forging ahead with valor, getting the new stuff done.

EVERY LITTLE BIT HELPS

There is an Italian expression I like very much, which is *tutto fa brodo*. Literally translated it means, "Everything makes soup." The intended meaning is "every little bit helps." When you are decorating the change throughout the long Middle, indeed every little bit helps. Any energy you put into decorating the change helps make it more clear to people that they are safe to move forward. And because these things are in the language of the community, you never know which ones will have the most impact. So, it's important to try a lot of different stuff. *Tutto fa brodo.*

NEXT

As a leader, *you* need to keep communicating too. What is your plan to share the strategy in a way that people get and makes them believe that you are serious this time?

CHAPTER 25

Top-Down Communications

Why People Do and Don't Listen

While it is most important to foster conversation about your strategy among the people doing the work and to decorate the change to keep it highly visible, as we talked about in the last two chapters, top-down communication from the leader is also necessary.

Top-down communication is not enough on it's own, but it's very important as a leader to show up consistently and make your presence and your personal commitment to the transformation felt. Your communications make your own personal engagement tangible and visible through the long Middle—it's another one of the things that decorate the change.

WHAT EVERYONE IS THINKING

I'm listening to this guy talk about this new thing, but I wonder. . . . What does he really believe? Is this transformation really his idea, or is he being forced to do this by the company? Is he really serious, or is this just more big talk about change that will never happen? Are we really going to do it? I doubt it. I will watch and see what he does next. If I don't see him talking about this again soon, I just won't worry about it . . .

Your organization is watching you. You have the chance to be highly present and consistent, or absent or haphazard, in your communications. Even if you have done an excellent job in creating conversations and decorating the change, your people need to hear directly from you too.

A critical action in implementing your strategy is that you are communicating about it continuously over the entire course of executing it.

Getting Initial Buy-in

Here are some critical steps to follow to make sure that people believe you and that they know you are serious—and more importantly, that they realize you are saying something that applies to them!

Remember They Are Not Really Listening

As we talked about in Chapter 23: Conversation, when you first talk about your strategy, your best assumption is that people are not listening. So first and foremost:

Your initial goal is not to sell the strategy—it's to give people a reason to listen.

To give them a reason to listen, you need to break through their fear and skepticism. Here are some useful steps to do that.

Set Context

Make it a point to share the context. What made you choose to change something or do something in the first place? Take the time to explain it.

As the leader, you live in the big picture. But the people in your organization live in the work.

You need to communicate the big picture and sell the business reasons why your strategy is important, and why the new thing must be done. Talk about the business pressures and drivers that caused you to develop the strategy. Make it vividly clear that the new way is vastly better than the current way—and why.

It's very important to remember that all the employees were not in on the planning.

Don't make the mistake of thinking your people can internalize a new strategy after hearing it one time. *You* didn't.

You, on the other hand, have been thinking about this strategy, and the importance of it, for a long time. This is an issue for many leaders. They have a tendency to think that everybody understands what they, themselves, understand. It doesn't seem necessary to invest a lot of effort in sharing the information because it seems so obvious to you.

What Is *Not* Changing

This may be the most important part of your change message. You are very focused on communicating about the change, but hearing what is *not* changing is the key that unlocks people's ability to be open to listening to something new. It lets them start listening from a position of, *Hey, I already know this; this isn't so scary.*

No one can take on brand new information if it is ALL brand new information.

By having some patience, and starting with saying, "Here are the things that are not changing," you give them a safe and confident place to stand. You give them a fighting chance of opening up to receive your new information. Never skip this part. Even if everything is changing, find something to talk about that stays the same. You will greatly increase your ability to execute if you do not skip this step. Even if pretty much everything is changing, you can resort to saying, "One thing that is not changing is that I am still here, and you can count on me." If that is the only thing that is not changing, still say that!

Thank Them for the Work So Far

Don't get so excited about the new stuff that you forget to thank people for the work that got you to this point. It really pisses people off to hear you go on about the great new strategy and feel like their past three years of hard work don't count for anything anymore. Even if the strategy requires you to throw away 100 percent of the work that has been done to this point, it is not a reason *not* to say thank you and acknowledge what they have been doing: "Thank you for the hard work that got us to this point." It is another door opener to get people ready to listen.

Keep It Simple

Make sure you can fit the basic points of your strategy on one page/slide/screen. **Even better, test yourself by telling your strategy to your mother. If she can't understand your basic strategy, your message is too complicated.**

No offense to very well-informed mothers, but we all have a way of overcomplicating our strategies. You should be able to communicate your strategy to someone who knows nothing about your business by answering a few simple questions: Who are we targeting? Why will we win? What problems do we have to overcome to do this? I help leaders simplify the descriptions of their strategies all the time. Having a simple way to describe your strategy doesn't mean your strategy is not deep and rich and brilliant and complicated; it means that you really know what you are doing and how to communicate it to others.

Strive to make the explanation of your strategy simple!

Here Is What the New Thing Means to You . . . Specifically

It's really important to anticipate people's questions and address them head on, in *their* words. Don't use lofty, impressive sounding business-speak. Don't avoid the real and uncomfortable questions people have.

One time I was a GM and had to greet the employees for the first time of a company that we were going to acquire. I said, "Hello, you all know why we are here; I'll get to all that in a moment, but I know that what you are all thinking is: *Do I still have a job? When will I know? And if I still do have a job, is it one that I will like? I didn't choose to work in a big company, and now I am stuck in a big company . . . if I even have a job. What will happen to me?*"

It wasn't hard to know that these were the questions that people would have. And by starting there, I helped them be ready to listen. I can promise you that if I started talking about the market opportunity for the merged product lines, no one would have been listening.

If you don't know what people are thinking and worried about, ask. Find out. During a challenging transformation I was leading, on a monthly all-hands webinar we included a "Heard in the Hallways" section. We would poll the employee base to hear what they were most confused, concerned, or upset about, and we'd bring those questions up so that I could address them. We sought to learn what they personally cared about on purpose, so that we could engage them personally. And we made sure not to clean the language up. We kept the questions in the language that they were asked. If you answer the questions in the same style and language they come in, you will earn a tremendous amount of respect, and people will be more open to really listen.

REGULAR UPDATES FROM YOU, THE LEADER

Consistency is a very powerful thing. I learned this when I was in my first sizable corporate management role. I wanted to keep my team updated about what I was thinking and doing and deciding. I also wanted to let them know that I noticed and appreciated specific things that they were accomplishing. Since I was very overscheduled and traveling a lot, I was concerned that if I didn't commit to something regular, my good intentions to communicate may get lost awash the sometimes crushing demands and activities competing for my time.

I Committed to Doing a Weekly Update

In each update I shared the news of the week and things I came across that I thought were interesting or important. I sent it to my team, and I sent it to my peers and my boss. It became known as "Patty's Friday update." Today I would do this with an internal blog with text and video.

I was genuinely surprised at how much people appreciated these updates. I got so much positive feedback.

People felt informed: They told me that because of this regular update they felt included. They knew what was important. They knew what decisions had been made and how key questions had been answered. It made them feel safe, that they could count on having current information each week.

People felt connected: They felt part of the bigger team. They had confidence in the strategy because it was reinforced (decorated) each week. They knew what issues we were addressing on a weekly basis—which helped them focus. They were in the loop.

People felt motivated: They knew what successes we achieved—which made them happy and proud. And they felt acknowledged and appreciated.

As I'll talk more about in Chapter 27: Sharing Information, people like to feel in the loop—a lot.

Good Communications Spread Confidence

Additionally, my peers thought, *Hey, this is a pretty good update,* and ended up forwarding it to their teams as well! Patty's Friday update became "a thing."

In fact, the weekly update was so well received that I did Patty's Friday update every week, faithfully, for 17 years! *I can't overstate the positive effect and business benefit that regularly sharing what you are thinking about as a leader has on your team.*

Informal Is Fine

Doing a regular update doesn't need to turn into a big, formal, over-whelming effort. In fact, it's much better if it doesn't. I think we've all seen the overproduced, highly corporate employee newsletters that are far from useful and motivating. That is not what I'm recommending. What people heard from me in these updates was whatever I could think of in 10 minutes on a Friday afternoon. I eventually got in the habit of recording some bullet points throughout the week, and asking my direct reports for input by Friday morning—so it was a very easy thing to do and maintain. And it also motivated good conversation, because people across the organization began to campaign to get their things into the Friday update. It had an unintended benefit of creating conversation in the right places.

Just Start

If you're thinking about doing this, just do it. Don't start by trying to create a media empire. Send a brief personal email, or better yet, use a blog that will take on a life of its own—in a good way. Let contributions happen organically in the beginning, then seek more regular input once you get in the rhythm of doing it at all. If you start out by making this a formal task for 15 people, you will stall before you start.

Don't Skip! Consistency Is Vital

I also learned that the regularity of the Friday update was even more important than the content. Once I started doing this, I skipped one. The backlash was remarkable. Rumors started flying: "Are we getting shut down? Is Patty leaving the company? Should we still keep working on this new thing?"

Whenever I would poll people regarding whether I should skip it when I had no real news, the resounding feedback was: "Don't skip." I learned that people would rather get minimal content then get no Friday update at all. People felt immediately nervous if I missed a week.

When you commit to communicating every week, some weeks you realize that there is not a lot to say! Some weeks I was truly scraping the bottom of the barrel for content. So every once in awhile my Friday update would be something content-free like: "Hi, this is Patty with the Friday update. I don't have any real news this week, but I just wanted to let you know that these two priorities we've been talking about are still key, and I want to thank you all for your hard work. So thank you and bye till next week."

Don't Be Intermittent

I learned that the predictability of the communication was the important part. The fact that I did it without fail every Friday turned the communication into an anticipated thing.

Everyone knew to watch for it.

Its regular appearance gave people confidence, and they paid more attention because it was anticipated on a schedule. If you communicate sporadically, people won't expect it, so they won't be looking for it, and might miss it. Although communicating sporadically is better than not communicating at all, the lack of predictability does not build momentum, and you'll lose a lot of the benefit. Trust and confidence will take a big hit.

Making People Feel Safe

It was fascinating to me that the regular heartbeat of the update in itself seemed to act as a signal to people that things were stable and that I, the leader, was truly engaged. Because I "showed up" for them personally every week, they could feel safe to be engaged too. This is an example of what I meant at the beginning of the chapter about showing up consistently and making your presence and your personal commitment to the transformation felt.

Get Help If You Need To

There is one caveat to my record. When I was running the HP OpenView organization of a few thousand people, I did the update every other week; and I hired a contractor to help me pull together key news and questions and provide me an outline to edit, and to which I could add my personal thoughts and language.

But it was still never a giant, overwhelming project for me or for the audience. And it was *so* worth it.

So, if you need to get someone to help you pull this together and prompt you to do it on a regular schedule, do it! Throughout the 17 years I did this, I did it sometimes on my own, sometimes with the help of an external person, and sometimes with the help of an internal person. I put in place whatever was required to make it happen, and then kept the effort up consistently. People like to feel like they are in the loop!

COMMUNICATE 21 TIMES

I think we all have the tendency to feel like we have communicated better than we actually have communicated. It takes quite a bit of effort for your audience to truly internalize your message. There is a well-tested marketing principle that says: *For your audience to understand and internalize your message well enough to act on it, it takes them hearing or seeing your message seven times. And for every one time they see or hear it, they have to be exposed to it three times.* That's 21 times!

I can tell you without question or hesitation, 21 times is not overkill.

If this amount of marketing communication is necessary for someone to take action to buy an electronic device or take a vacation, at least this much is necessary to get them to internalize and act on a business strategy!

You Need to Be Unfailingly Consistent in Your Communications

Only when you are mind-numbingly bored with talking about your strategy will your organization begin to feel confident about acting on it.

Your consistent, repetitive communications along with rich conversations among the people doing the work will ensure that confidence in you as the leader remains high, and that progress does not stall.

One of the very useful elements of this type of regular communication is the "communication timeline" we talked about in Chapter 3: Timing and Momentum. Each time you are consistent with your communication, one less person will be asking "Are we still doing this?" and will just start doing it.

Show That the Leadership Team Is Aligned

One last thing that makes a big difference it to recognize that your organization is watching the whole management team for clues about who is engaged or not. One way to undermine your transformation is to have your management team not be seen by the whole organization as communicating a coherent message and supporting the new thing the same way.

Even if your team really does agree, if they are not all sharing the fact that they are on board in a visible way by joining the conversation, those silences will spread skepticism faster than anything you can do proactively by what you alone are communicating.

Make it a managed plan that your organization is hearing from your whole management team. In my experience, this in itself is worthy of fueling conversation across the team: "Wow, they are all saying this same thing!" This won't happen unless you do it on purpose.

Here is an example. When I was leading a large transformation that affected about 3,000 people across the world, my staff was about 12 people who worked in many different countries. We committed to doing a webinar every month and at each one, every staff member was on the phone. At the beginning of the webinar, everyone on the leadership team would say hello, describe where they were in the world and what time it was, and make a short comment on a particular theme of our transformation. This was very powerful. Even more important than the specifics of what they each said, the resounding message to the employee base was: "I'm here again this month, I am present and in support of this transformation." They showed that they cared by showing up. This then made their teams feel safe to engage.

Next

How can you make sure you, as the leader, are hearing the information, successes, and risks most critical to your transformation?
   Read on . . .

CHAPTER 26

Listen on Purpose

Finding the Insights That Make You Brilliant

WHAT EVERYBODY IS THINKING

We have a new manager. I wonder what she is like? I wonder what she is thinking? Does she even know what we do? Why does the opinion of someone from the outside always mean more than everything we know? Does she really know what she is doing? Is she going to make changes? Is it going to be painful? Do I trust this person? I don't know whether to support this person, or to just keep my head down, or to start looking for a new job . . .

NEVER COUNT ONLY ON FILTERED INFORMATION

I learned an important lesson when I was in my first big leadership role. When stepping in to lead the team, I was the suspicious, new person from outside. Although I had a pretty good, big-picture plan for what I wanted to accomplish, I admit I was thinking, *Hmmm, but what* exactly *should I be doing? Where should I start?*

My first thought was to look at the roles and the work of all the people who reported to me and start trying to optimize that in one way or another, but I knew in my gut that that was not the right answer. That was their job. I knew I should be driving strategy that spanned the whole organization—but what would that look like exactly on Tuesday?

I was lucky to have a mentor who told me the secret: "Talk to everybody and you'll know what to do."

Really? Everybody?

So I talked to everybody.

In my first two weeks on the job I did eighty one-on-one meetings. It was exhausting! But it was hugely enlightening. I can tell you—before all those conversations, my go-forward strategy was really fuzzy, and after all those conversations I knew exactly what to do.

The scary and notable part was that if I had not done these meetings, I would have had no idea what the most vital issues to work on really were. I would have gotten bogged down in the way the organization was currently working, instead of discovering how I needed to improve it. I would not have discovered what my job really was.

> **When you talk to the people doing the work,**
> **you discover things you will never learn from**
> **your managers.**

It's not that your managers are maliciously hiding information from you, but if you never experience the business from the perspective of the people doing the work—the product developers, the sales reps, and the service people—you truly won't know what business you are in. You won't know what you need to be fixing, improving, inventing, or stopping.

For example, a big source of insight came to me from going on customer visits. I came to relish customer visits—not for the customer contact, but for the ride in the car with the sales rep! I learned more about what business I was in by these rides to and from the airport than I could ever learn by talking to my team back at headquarters. Talking to the people doing the work will always show you something important about the way forward.

Ask everyone in your organization, "What should we be doing better or different? What should we start or stop doing? How am I doing?"

See What You Are Missing

Once I started talking to individuals I realized some important things I wasn't seeing from the official management chain. For example:

- I learned that there was one manager in my organization who was a bully. This manager was great at managing up, so I couldn't have seen it without talking to the team.

- I learned that there were three different projects that were duplicate efforts. I didn't see this because my managers weren't talking to each other about it! So that was two problems to solve, the duplication and the team's collaboration.

- I learned that employees were frustrated that a decision had not been made, and they were spinning their wheels waiting for direction. But the decision had been made, so I learned that I had a communication issue.

None of this information was coming up through my direct staff.

KEEP YOUR TEAM ON TRACK THROUGH THE MIDDLE

As a leader, you can use the critical insight you gain from talking to individuals about what's really happening to improve the business and to keep things on track throughout the Middle. You will be surprised just how useful the information is, and how much more effective a leader you will become once you know this information.

You can't keep your organization focused through the Middle if you don't understand what is tripping people up, what they are worried about, and what obstacles they are facing on a personal level.

And you will never truly understand these things if you only talk to your direct reports. You have to talk to everybody.

As my roles grew to lead organizations of thousands, I could no longer talk to everybody but I still made sure to put time in my schedule to talk to the people doing the work, either one-on-one or in groups. I did this every week.

GET ACCESS TO THE BEST IDEAS

Another reason to always be listening on purpose is to make sure that you are putting yourself in the stream of the very best ideas.

One of the most critical factors in creating big success is imagination. What if the thing that will create your biggest success is something you haven't thought of yet? What if the best solution to the problem you are working on is something you are not likely to think of on your own? **You can't do something remarkable if you never think of it!**

Highly successful people are always ready to learn from anyone. They seek out good ideas everywhere, all the time, and when they find one it doesn't matter if it comes from a highly paid consultant or the person that comes in to clean up after lunch. They recognize good ideas, they adopt them, and they thank people for them. This openness, generosity, appreciation, and acknowledgment makes people want to help them. So, they have a bigger and much steadier source of good ideas than people who either don't think they can learn from others, or refuse to acknowledge when they do.

I have worked with many people whose egos prevent them from ever saying, "Wow, that's a good idea, I never thought of that, thank you." It's such a shame, because they are dismissing a very deep and broad source of valuable insights. The people who need to act like they know everything and have a need to be the only ones who can have good ideas in reality don't get very far. *They get to act like a big shot for a little while, but never actually become a big shot!*

BUILDING YOUR PIPELINE OF GOOD IDEAS

Here are some things you can do:

1. Create a habit of talking to people in the beginning, before you get near the end of the process of what you are doing, or before you feel like you know all the answers.

2. Start conversations assuming you know *less* than the other person. Even if you are certain that you know more, put yourself in this mindset and take some time to really listen anyway.

3. Catch yourself from saying, "We tried that already" or "We already thought of that"—that shuts off the flow. Instead, ask "In that case, how would you deal with this complication?"

4. Talk to people you don't ordinarily talk to. Ask them what they are thinking about—you'll be surprised how many new ideas this will generate.

5. Ask around for people who do similar work and seek out best practices. (Secret: This is a great way to ask for help without looking like you don't know what you are doing!)

6. Specifically seek out people who think very differently from you and meet with them regularly to discuss your work, your plans, and your goals.

My most inspiring successes have almost all started from someone else's idea!

That is the truth! My biggest breakthroughs in my work and my career required me to do things that were simply not in my imagination before someone else put them there—or I never imagined that it was something possible for me. For example, I went for my biggest promotions because mentors told me I was ready, not because I knew it myself.

It doesn't matter where a good idea comes from. Just be sure to put yourself in the stream and recognize and appreciate them when they come along!

ARE YOU LISTENING?

I made a huge error once when it came to listening and learned an important lesson.

When I was running a very large global organization, I had a 360-degree evaluation done, which included feedback from all the levels and geographies of my organization. When I got the results, I was shocked (and heartbroken) to learn that the people in the lower levels of the organization (everyone doing the work) all scored me as a terrible listener. I didn't get a medium score; I got the lowest score!

I really couldn't believe it at first. My coach reminded me of the difference between intention and behavior. While I got that concept, and I admitted to being guilty of a gap between intentions and behaviors in some other areas, I argued that I really do invest significant effort into the behavior of being a good, patient, and active listener.

So after some reflection, we determined the real issue. It was not a problem with my listening intentions, skills, or behaviors, it was that the vast majority of my organization never got to experience me listening! Since they never saw me in action listening, they gave me a poor grade.

So I changed my priorities. I made sure that each week I prioritized a minimum of six hours per week for listening. I created webpages for feedback, and I held breakfast meetings with groups of employees. I reported out on what I was hearing.

I created listening opportunities that everyone could observe and participate in. I broadened the conversation to include Everyone.

Some Leaders Resist Listening

I see many leaders resist doing this type of listening to everyone for a few reasons:

1. They are concerned that they are going around the managers who report to them, and this feels wrong.
2. Their ego tells them, "I am a big shot, so I don't talk to the people doing the work, I only talk to other big shots."
3. They are afraid of what they will hear, or that they will lose credibility if word of the broken things in their own organization is spoken aloud.
4. They think they don't have time to do this.

I hate to break the news, but if ugly issues are already being spoken of, you will definitely lose credibility if you're the only one who doesn't know about them!

It's so important to stay connected to reality. It is always very sad when I talk to a leader who tells me, "Everything is fine," and then people above, around, and below him tell me that this leader is terrible and doesn't have a clue. Actually, I could guess that up front, because any time a leader says, "Everything is fine," I know they are either lying or they are clueless!

Everything is never fine.

These leaders are seldom in their jobs a year later.

You simply can't do your job without knowing the things you learn from these conversations. You can act like a big shot all you want, and pretend you are above having conversations with product developers and sales and service staff, but you will be missing a vital source of real information that will ultimately come back to surprise you in a bad way.

Make it part of the culture that you are going to spend time talking to individuals. As long as you don't start directly assigning work to individuals without involving their managers, the managers will not be offended or concerned by your having these conversations. And the people will be really motivated by it!

And as far as time goes . . . you don't have time *not* to do this. Sure, if you bother to ask, and care enough to know the truth, you will face some conflict and learn issues that make you uncomfortable as a leader. I was sometimes mortified to learn of truly screwed up things that were happening in parts of my organization "under my watch." But better to know them and choose what to fix than to assume everything is fine and get even further out of touch with reality.

NEXT

How well does your organization share information across groups? How will you make sure that everyone is getting the information they need to do their jobs? Read on . . .

CHAPTER 27

Sharing Information

Communicating Across
Organizational Silos

PEOPLE FEEL UNINFORMED

When I do strategy execution work with executive teams, I typically begin with an assessment phase where I talk with people across the organization at multiple levels. So I end up talking to a lot of people across a lot of levels in a lot of organizations. One issue I hear pretty universally is about silos. People feel uninformed about what is happening in other organizations.

WHAT EVERYONE IS THINKING

1. *I thought you were doing that:* So important tasks are dropped.
2. *I didn't know you were doing that:* So work is duplicated.
3. *I don't know what I should be doing:* So motivation is low; work stalls.
4. *I didn't realize we knew/decided that:* So bad calls are made when things that are actually known are not widely used.
5. *I don't know the priorities:* So wrong work is done. Effort is wasted. And needed work is not done.

Keeping momentum through the Middle requires a constant sharing of information across your organization, so people can feel safe that what they are doing makes sense in the context of what everyone else is doing.

Bridging Across Silos

Pretty much every organization struggles with siloed information. I have been so surprised to see the existence of silos even in very small organizations. I've seen this even in startups where there are only four people and one of them will say something like, "I need to get marketing to agree." Seriously, marketing? You mean Bob?

> **Silos form no matter what the size and complexity of an organization is, and the only way to get information moving is to get it moving on purpose.**

People tend to forget to communicate with people outside their own groups. For example, when I was running a global marketing organization, every day back at headquarters someone would bring me a plan or a proposal and want my approval or opinion, and I would say, "What have the people in Europe and Asia said about this?" Every day— for more than a year—I had to ask the same question: "What have the people in Europe and Asia said about this?" It is a tough habit to break to get people to share information with colleagues who they don't see everyday.

Everyone: Share What You Know

Getting people to share what they know is critical. When I work with leaders on this, I get them to make lists of all the people and groups they should be sharing information with, and all of the people and groups they should be seeking information from.

> **It is natural not to share what we each know on our own; it is not interesting to us—because we already know it!**

We all take what we already know for granted. But people who are in other groups or other sites would love to know what we know! Headquarters would love to know what great things happened to customers or in regional branches. People in remote geographies would love to be in the loop on what is getting decided in corporate. Why is this so hard?

By first making these lists, people get reminded that there are others who exist out there in the organization who would benefit from knowing what they know. Anything you can do to make this happen on purpose is a good thing.

People like to feel that they are in the loop!

THE BIG "AHA"

A while back I got a huge "aha" about why this is so hard and how to do it right. I want to share something I learned when I was visiting my alma mater, Monmouth University.

IDEA TO REVENUE IN 16 WEEKS

Monmouth offers a remarkable class in entrepreneurship.

The very impressive thing about this class is that in a 16-week semester, the students conceive of and implement a business, and get it to the point of generating revenue. Most of these businesses continue to grow beyond the semester, and turn into successful businesses that graduating students run, or they get spun out into larger existing businesses.

Sixteen weeks to revenue. Wow! When I was talking to the professor, I asked, "How on Earth do you do that? You have an amazing track record of getting these upstart businesses to revenue so quickly. What do you attribute that to?"

He told me that a big part of it is "the way we communicate." He talked about the importance of communication and particularly the importance of shared information across groups in a fast-growing business.

So I asked him how they managed communication across the "company."

Structured Communication

He told me that at the beginning of the semester, at the launch of the business, the class splits into functional business groups: marketing, sales, product development, infrastructure, and so on. Each team has a leader who acts as the manager for that group.

He then showed me a computer screen that looked something like the very non-flashy picture in Figure 27.1. He went on to explain, "This is how we communicate":

1. Every week the managers are required to post status updates about all the decisions, results, and open questions that exist in their areas. And they are required to respond to questions that come in on their updates.

2. Every week all the people in the rest of the organization are required to read all the updates, questions, and comments on their own function plus all the top-level updates from all the teams.

So for example, all the marketing people would need to read all marketing updates, as well as all of the marketing questions and discussions in their entirety, and then also read the top-level updates from sales, product development, and so forth.

ACME Business Overview:

⌖ **Marketing**
Updates
Comments and Questions

▼ **Sales**
Updates
Comments and Questions

⚗ **Product Development**
Updates
Comments and Questions

📦 **Manufacturing**
Updates
Comments and Questions

Figure 27.1   Company Communication Dashboard

JUST CRAZY ENOUGH TO WORK

My initial reaction was, *Why would every business on Earth not benefit from communicating in this way?* But here is the big "aha": The students shared information so well with one another because they were *being graded on it!*

1. Managers were being graded on producing regular communications.
2. Every single employee was being graded on consuming them.

In business, we don't typically grade anyone on sharing and consuming information—let alone grade everyone on it!

SHARING INFORMATION ON PURPOSE

The benefit of shared knowledge in a business is incredibly valuable, and the risk of not having it is incredibly high and very costly. But communication in the form of sharing knowledge is so often viewed by managers and employees as an extra, non-vital thing. It's outside the job description, and therefore, optional.

Why not make sharing information part of everyone's performance objectives, like the students who are being graded on it?

Wouldn't that be great? Every manager could have a performance check on every employee: How effectively have you shared information with your target groups? How effectively have you consumed information from your target groups? I actually don't think this is very hard to do.

INTERNAL SOCIAL SHARING TOOLS

The simple tool the class was using was a social sharing tool. The manager of each function posted their updates on something that works like a blog or a Facebook page.

The benefit of using a social sharing tool for these type of updates is that it collects, organizes, and archives status, decisions, questions, and conversations automatically—all in one place that any interested party can connect to and participate in.

If I were still in a corporate role I would set up this type of communication, and I would grade people on using it!

Here is what I would do:

1. I would have everyone who owned a key product, project, or program be the leader of the discussion forum for their program, and require them to post updates on an internal sharing (blog-like) platform.

2. They would need to invite their peers and everyone who should know about their project to connect to their stream.

3. I would also set an expectation that everyone should spend at least one hour per week reading relevant updates.

Save time and reduce email. Organizations who communicate this way also dramatically decrease their email load and waste far less time having their people searching for information. It's all collected and automatically archived.

No excuses for not knowing. There is never an excuse for not knowing information that is shared and archived, or a reason to blame management for not communicating. It's all there.

Lightweight is good. If a blog seems like heavy lifting or mysterious, think of each important program in your business having a page that works like a Facebook page, where leaders can post updates for all interested parties to see, review, and comment on.

Don't let people get scared off by thinking they need to turn into prolific writers. Brief is actually better, and bullet points are fine: five key points a week about what has been decided, finished, or changed, and what the open questions are. Regularly posted communication is a game changer. People will feel like they are in the loop. And while it may seem like extra work at the beginning, once it is rolling there will be far less wasted time. Find a way to make sharing information not optional. The payoff will be large.

NEXT

How will you make your employees feel truly empowered on a personal level so they will move mountains for you?
    Read on . . .

CHAPTER 28

Power and Trust

How to Make People Feel Like Superheroes

WHAT EVERYONE IS THINKING

I work super hard, and no one seems to notice. I'd like to be respected more. It's not clear to me that my job is really valued. I'm always a bit nervous about what might happen to me. I am a competent, interesting person with good ideas and nobody here really has my back.

HOW TO BUILD GENUINE LOYALTY AND NOT BE A JERK

I was very fortunate early in my career to meet a mentor who showed me that you could be a very successful business leader by respecting people and sharing power. There are many examples of executives that go the other way—*for me to win, you need to lose*. They hoard power and treat people like crap. I might have believed that was necessary without a good role model.

You can certainly have a form of success as a power hungry asshole, but thankfully it's not a requirement (and does not fit my definition of success). I also believe that building a strong team that feels acknowledged and respected is a much more reliable approach to achieving success because it gives you more real power in the end.

I built my own career from entry level engineering and marketing positions up through many levels, ultimately becoming a CEO, by sharing power.

"Imagined-Power" People

Here is a way to think about what I refer to as "imagined power." People often ask me if it was hard for me to go from running really large organizations to having my own (implied—"much smaller") company. This was never an issue for me because I always maintained a psychological distance between the *power of my role* (managing a $1B+ global business with a multi-hundred-million dollar budget and thousands of people) and *my own personal power*.

I took responsibility for the power of the large role very seriously, but I never pretended that I personally owned that power.

So when I stepped out of a huge business into a small business, it was not difficult for me to adjust, because I was still the same me. (Just as a note, I will say that it was interesting to watch other people adjust to my change in perceived power status. There were several people who I thought were real friends when I had position power, who dropped me like a stone when I did not. Ugly.)

When I see leaders who claim this big role power as their own personal power, I refer to this as "imagined power." An executive role is hard enough without constant investment to maintain a false facade of personal power that doesn't actually exist. It's exhausting. And in the end it's actually less powerful in ways that matter to your success and the success of your business.

As an example, I am thinking of one executive in particular who exemplified this behavior. She was a C-level direct report to the CEO of a Fortune 50 company. She was meeting me and my peers, who were at the time C-level direct reports to the CEO of a smaller company. Her dismissive demeanor made it immediately clear that she saw us as *very far beneath her* on the food chain.

I remember thinking when I met her: *Wow, you are trying really hard to make sure you come across as a big, scary executive that is making sure we know our place beneath you. That must be exhausting!*

I wondered, is this because . . .

1. You are insecure and have a need to make people feel like you are more powerful than they are?

2. You were taught, or simply believe, that this is the way a big executive is supposed to treat others?

3. You are so self-involved that you don't even realize that you are so thoroughly dismissing people?

4. You actually believe that you are a superior life form?

I never know which of these is at play when I meet one of these executives. But I always feel that they are confusing the power of their role with their own personal power.

"REAL-POWER" PEOPLE AND RESPECT

Conversely, the leaders who inspired me the most were the ones who did not get caught up in personal power. They were the ones who built true business power by engaging and respecting employees at all levels (Everyone). They were the ones who, even though they were far above me organizationally, would sit across the table and talk to me as an equal. They'd say things like, "This is a tough business we are in! What are you seeing out there? What do you think I should do?" They were interested. They were open. They were always learning.

Real Business Power

If you acknowledge that you have a big responsibility—because you are in a powerful role—but you share power and respect with others, you will build a loyal and powerful team that supports you. So you actually gain real power in your business—much bigger power than you can create if you try to own the power yourself. And this is so critical in a transformation!

> **I'd rather have 100 peoples' worth of positive power and genuine loyalty than to try to build my own power by keeping 100 people down. It is exhausting to even think about!**

I always choose the road of helping people thrive, and sharing power is fundamental to that. Here are some practical ways that I have seen the difference play out, so you can get an idea of where you want to land.

Human vs. Boss If the thinking starts with *we are both humans* vs. *I am the boss and you are the worker*, you create an environment where everyone feels acknowledged. If you flaunt special privileges that only the boss gets, people will feel resentful and will not bring their best to the business.

If you make an investment to spend personal time with people in the trenches, on the assembly line, on the help desk, or literally in the trenches (if your business digs trenches), you show that you understand and value all the jobs in your organization and you are not "above it all." It builds tremendous loyalty (with Everyone) because when you ask someone to do work for you, they know that you appreciate what you are asking them to do. It is hard to overestimate the value of this as a leader.

Curious vs. Right People protecting their power tend to need to be right and to stay right. So it's not just that they are not good listeners, they actually have a need to not listen—because what they hear might threaten their "right-ness" and therefore their power facade. Leaders who share power are genuinely open and curious. They invite new ideas and are always learning. They learn what is really going on in their organizations and therefore know what is causing inefficiency, frustration, and suffering—so they can fix it.

The "always-right" executive doesn't want to hear it. They are right often enough that they can succeed, but they miss the opportunity to recognize breakthroughs that others might contribute. And they totally miss the opportunity to build motivation and support to have a truly loyal team to help them when things get tough.

Promote Others vs. Inflate Yourself Leaders who solely take personal credit for their organizations' work are again trying to hold on to false personal power. Leaders who promote and elevate the stars within their team build a much higher value organization. Leaders who share power often hire people better than themselves and give them support to excel. Then they give them recognition and help them move up. The whole organization gets stronger. I talked more about this in Chapter 10: The People.

Open vs. Secret   People protecting false personal power tend to be very secretive. They believe that if they know more than everyone else, they will remain very important.

Leaders who share power communicate a lot. They make it a point to share as much information as possible with everybody. They see additional power in having a well-informed team that can contribute more because they know more, a team who is motivated to contribute more because they feel respected.

Respect vs. Money   Another trait I have seen with leaders protecting their personal power is that they pay people more money than they could make elsewhere, with a key requirement of the job being: *Don't question me, stay in your place, and make me look good. Build up my ego by being at my beck and call. I pay you a lot, I deserve your unwavering and constant availability and adoration. Don't complain if I act like I don't respect you. That's what all the money is for.*

"Shared-power" leaders win people over by building an environment of trust and respect. They create meaning for people so they can feel proud of their work. They offer personal recognition. They go out of their way to make the work matter to the people doing it.

TREAT PEOPLE LIKE PEOPLE

To truly motivate your organization and build loyalty and trust, it's important to treat people like people. It seems obvious to say it this way, but it is sadly frequent that I see leaders instead treating people like "resources." I've seen leaders call people "resources" to their faces. I've also seen leaders relate to their direct staff as people, but then refer to their outsourced organizations in other parts of the world as "resources." We are all people.

And a key factor in treating people like people is to invest in learning what they truly care about, both at work and outside of work. When you start treating a person like a whole person instead of a cog in a work machine, you build the foundation for a huge amount of trust. And that trust drives motivation and momentum.

Don't Guess What People Care About, Ask Them

If you bother to ask what people really care about, you will be amazed at the answers and how many things there are that you can do (without money, by the way) that will make a material difference to them. Don't guess . . . ask! Don't do unto others as you would have them do unto you; do unto others in ways that they want. And know how to do this because you asked. Personally ask each person, "What is important to you? What do you truly care about?"

One time when I asked this question, a man in his fifties started crying. I asked him, "What's up?" and he said, "I'm sorry, I was just so surprised by this question because in my entire career, no one has ever asked!" As I talked about the value of unstructured conversation in Chapter 12, learning what people really think is a very powerful thing. Don't avoid it. Dive in.

> **The best managers I see really take the time to get to know their employees and to find out: What is really in this for you?**

I have a colleague who does this by focusing the conversation on "bragging rights" with his employees. He will say, "Job description aside, what do you want to be able to have on your resume or tell your friends a year from now?" He gets answers that range from "I really want to be a second level manager" to "I'd like to make sure I go to one exotic place every year so I can post cool pictures on my Facebook page." Some will say, "I want to be able to run a marathon." Others will say, "I want to be recognized as the expert in my field by the media." The important thing is that the answer is different for everybody. So you have to ask. Once you know, you can try to match projects and opportunities to people's wish lists. It's hugely motivating when you can line up a work project with something someone is already really motivated about on a personal level.

What is interesting about this conversation is that even if you can't give them what they specifically want in their jobs, or if the thing they care about is not work related, the fact that you had the conversation (and that you know what they care about) has the effect of making them feel more motivated because they feel like their true selves are recognized by the company. If you ask them periodically about this thing they are truly passionate about, they will feel like their passion is welcome at work—and you get a more engaged person at work. It's a whole lot better than not asking.

Acknowledge That People Have a Life Outside of Work

I love this example: I talked to an executive once who every few months took out the project plans for his team and invited everyone to put their personal events on the plan . . . weddings, graduations, school plays, and so on. I thought this was brilliant! He was acknowledging that people have lives that matter, and by putting the important personal dates on the work project plan it gave the whole team the opportunity to recognize each other's lives and come together to cover for people when they had important events. It was not a 100 percent guarantee that if you put a personal event on the work schedule that it would be accommodated, but the intention and the effort went a huge way to building trust.

When you acknowledge that people are not only work robots and that they have lives outside of work that matter, they become fiercely loyal to you. I often had situations where people needed to take time out of the workday to tend to personal matters, and I never questioned them because I knew that I could call them and count on them at any hour of the day if I needed to.

There was one instance I remember where someone worked two hours away from headquarters. In the normal course of events she would make the drive during business hours because at commute time the drive could be four or more hours with traffic! I never questioned, "So you're driving at 10 am," because in the normal course of events it did not matter. She was at the office plenty, and she got more than her share of work done. She delivered the results. But one day, there was an emergency on a Friday afternoon. I had to ask her to stay. I said, "I'm really sorry because I know the drive you have ahead of you, and I know I am ruining your evening by asking you to stay late this Friday, and I might even be ruining your weekend . . . but I really need you to stay and help me finish this." She didn't bat an eyelash. She simply said, "Of course" and got to work. If you allow people some slack and treat them like humans when scheduling is not vital, they will come through when it is.

CREATE A PROCESS FOR RECOGNITION

Another issue I find with building motivation and trust is that often people don't feel recognized. It is seriously de-motivating when someone does something extraordinary and heroic, and no one notices. It destroys trust not just for that person but for those around her.

The trouble that most organizations face is not that they are stingy with recognition; it's just that they don't have a way of knowing when good things happen. Everybody's busy. People travel and people work in different sites, so great work happens all the time and you just don't see it. How do you know when good things happen?

The good news is that this is really easy to fix. **The first step is to just make it clear to your team that you want to know when anyone in your organization does something remarkable.** This in itself inspires trust.

Create a simple process for any individual in any location to feed a suggestion for recognition of a peer or employee up the management chain—and then act on it.

MAKE IT PERSONAL

Commit to the idea that when a thank-you request comes in, an executive will personally say "thank you" to the individual. Spend time in every staff meeting on the topic of recognition. When someone deserves to be recognized, have an executive outside of their organization go say "thank you" personally. Ask the GM to make a phone call or send a handwritten note. (I did not say email on purpose. Email is the least personal way to thank someone.) These days, a handwritten note is like a work of art! It definitely stands out.

Recognition is easy and inexpensive to do. Build a habit of recognition in your organization that will make people feel appreciated for carrying their share of the load decisively through the Middle.

MAKE PEOPLE FEEL LIKE SUPERHEROES

I want to share this message I received from a former employee to make a final point about sharing power and building motivation: "Patty, When I worked for you, I thought I was Superman."

It was wonderful to get that message. But additionally, those 11 words sum up for me, in a pretty profound way, what I believe being a good leader of a high performing team is about.

He continued: "I have occasionally reflected on why that was. Not sure I know all the answers, but the things I do know are that the environment was real, the energy was high, and the crap was low."

If you set out with the goal to create an environment where your people can feel amazing, you'll be on a really good track.

A great control point measure for your own leadership is: How many of my people feel like superheroes? The simple approach is this: Share power. Hire top people, give them big work, support them, step back, and let them be amazing. Don't just delegate work. Delegate power. Let people make decisions and solve problems. Let them do great work they can be proud of, and help them get recognized for it. If you hire top performers, show them trust and respect, and make sure they get the credit; they will move mountains for you. Get out of their way!

People like to be amazing. Let them.

YOU CAN'T ACHIEVE A TRANSFORMATION WITHOUT TRUST

Virtually all of the things I've talked about in this book are steps that will result in building trust. From being concrete and consistent about outcomes, control points, measures, and timelines to being clear about resources, making the right organizational and people decisions, communicating clearly about performance, eliminating uncertainty, supporting the transformation with unfailingly consistent valor, communicating consistently, and fostering conversation . . . all of these things serve to build trust.

Every day, as a leader, you need to be doing things to actively build trust, and if you follow the MOVE model (**M**iddle-**O**rganization-**V**alor-**E**veryone), you will be on the right track.

Most people are pro-trust. You don't see people walking around saying that they don't think trust is important, or that they think trust is a bad thing. But what you do see is that many leaders take trust for granted. They don't think about trust in a way that they believe they must do things on purpose to build or maintain trust. They don't see trust as an action item.

The thing about trust is that there is no neutral. You are either building trust or you are destroying it.

If you do nothing, trust will bleed out of the system because people will not see you showing up, personally doing and investing in the things that build trust. Even if you are not doing anything bad, you are still letting trust degrade by your inaction—without a specific focus on building trust, your transformation is not likely to get done well, on time, or at all.

Building trust is not a "nice to have"; it's directly related to the bottom line and the success of your transformation. For people to be engaged and motivated, and to do stuff, they have to feel safe. And to feel safe, they need to feel trust. Trust is the necessary fuel for motivation for your organization to drive the journey through the long Middle. Without trust, people will not be personally motivated, they will stall and delay, they will not be creative, and they will not care if they produce low-quality products and services, annoy customers, or deliver late.

The reality is that when people feel trusted and they trust you, they will work harder and faster, be more innovative, get more done, and treat customers better. They will trust you when they are in the Middle and can't yet see the light at the end of the tunnel. They will keep going. They will MOVE.

ACKNOWLEDGMENTS

First of all, a giant thank you to my mentors. I would not have arrived here and written this book if it were not for you. I can never thank you enough, but here is one more feeble attempt . . . THANK YOU: Jim Davis, Al Fasola, Webb McKinney, Bill Russell, and Duane Zitzner.

Next, thank you to my advisory board. You always have my back. You provide so many insights. Your fingerprints are all in this book: Al Fasola, Bob Kaplan, Sandor Kovacs, Brian Kilcourse, Joanna Kulesa, Barbara Nelson, Resa Pearson, and Richard Walker.

Now on to the many people who inspired the ideas in this book and who helped it come to life by sharing insights, metaphors, quotes, and examples; people whose stories I told in the book; people I learned these lessons from; and people who helped me along the way: Jonathan Adams, Jill Ambrose, Paul and Chrisna Avenant, Linda Beardsley, Paul Beavers, Paul Beiser, Brian Bergdoll, Andy Burtis, John Buzza, Eric Carrasquilla, Pam Cass, Cindy Clarke, Steve Diamond, Beth Devin, Julie Dubas, John Fernandez, Cathy FitzGerald, Nancy Friedman, Nelson Gonzales, Nick Goss, Jim Grant, Don Joos, Scott Jordan, Ben Kiker, Carol Kruse, Mark Lieberman, Heidi Lorenzen, Brad Maihack, Katherine Mancuso, Andrea Masina, Paul Muller, Jim McDonnell, Mike McGrorey, Marc McKenzie, Meta Mehling, Rob Meinhardt, Vonda Mills, Dhiren Pardhanani, John Peters, Dale Predmore, Suzanne Pherigo, Ramona Pierson, Stuart Rakley, William Reeves, Kay Rhodes, Stephanie Robinson, Liz Saiz, Rich Sanzi, Jan Silverman, Stan Slap, Bill Sudlow, Jessica Swank, Tom Tiernan, Tiffany Tuell, Mary Tinkcom, Tom Viola, Thomas Volk, Jacek Walicki, Dave Wright, Jim Zafarana, and Nitza Zuppas.

Also, thank you to the members of Azzarello Group, my professional development program. Our monthly webinars and Coaching Hour calls give me so many ideas and new insights about what leaders deal with. Many of the ideas in this book stemmed from our conversations. I hope you know that I get value from these exchanges too. Thank you.

I also must acknowledge the dark side. There were so many people who inspired the ideas in this book by being the bad examples: the bullies, the egomaniacs, the terrible communicators, the inconsistent leaders—those who had a total lack of valor and could not make a decision or stick to anything. You showed me the way forward by creating the examples of how things go very wrong. I learned a lot from you and from what happened and didn't happen in your organizations, and the havoc and damage you wreaked for the business and the people. I thank you for the learning, and will in return leave you unnamed!

Finally, I want to thank the people who helped me in the review and production of this book: Thank you to Andrew Binstock, Eric Carrasquilla, Jim Davis, Al Fasola, Ben Kiker, Brian Kilcourse, Marc McKenzie, and Jacek Walicki for your insights and feedback. And many thanks to the editorial and production team at John Wiley & Sons for bringing this book into the world: Richard Narramore, Deborah Schindlar, Peter Knox, Paul McCarthy, and Tiffany Colon.

RESOURCES

Here are some other resources and programs that you might find useful.

1. **My website and blog:** www.PattyAzzarello.com.

2. **My other book:** *RISE: 3 Practical Steps for Standing Out as a Leader, Advancing Your Career AND Liking Your Life* (Ten-Speed Press, 2012). Available in stores and online.

3. **Speaking:** To book a speaking engagement with me for your internal or customer event, contact info@PattyAzzarello.com.

4. **Membership to Azzarello Group for professional development:** I offer a membership program for business leaders to get advice and coaching directly from me on a monthly basis through webinars and member Coaching Hour conference calls. This program is open to individuals and corporate groups. See www.AzzarelloGroup.com for more information.

5. **Strategy into Action program for business execution:** In this program I use the MOVE model with clients to help them optimize the execution of their strategy. I can work with you and your executive team on site with strategy sessions and workshops. For more information on this program see www.PattyAzzarello.com/strategy.

6. **Manager training—leadership development workshops:** My leadership development programs reinforce the concepts in the MOVE model and help your mid-level managers get ready to step up to think and work more strategically, increase their accountability and engagement, and lead their teams to implement your transformation. For more information on this see www.PattyAzzarello.com/leadership.

7. **Contact:** You can contact me online:

- Website: www.PattyAzzarello.com/contact
- Facebook: Patty Azzarello Practical Business Ideas for Humans @facebook/AzzarelloPatty
- Twitter: @PattyAzzarello
- LinkedIn: PattyAzzarello

ABOUT THE AUTHOR

Patty Azzarello is an accomplished business leader and an expert at getting organizations to function better and execute their strategies. She is a former CEO and general manager who has personally led multiple business transformations and turnarounds, and has built several highly successful management teams.

Currently, Patty is the CEO and founder of Azzarello Group, Inc., serving companies in diverse industries across the world to get better at what they do, through speaking engagements, strategy sessions, and leadership workshops. She is sought after as a business adviser for her unique and practical perspective on what makes people and organizations function (or not) and how to engage organizations at all levels to create more business value.

Patty holds degrees in electronic engineering and computer science from Monmouth University. She started her career as an engineer and moved up through the ranks, ultimately becoming a general manager and a CEO. She has also held executive leadership positions in product development, marketing, and sales. She became the youngest general manager at Hewlett-Packard at the age of 33, and was running a billion dollar software business by the age of 35. She was a CEO for the first time at the age of 38.

Her refreshing, nonacademic, experienced-based style and approach enable her clients to move forward decisively. She inspires confidence and action, and does it with much respect and a sense of humor. Patty is also the author of the best-selling book *RISE: 3 Practical Steps to Advancing Your Career, Standing Out as a Leader AND Liking Your Life* (TenSpeed Press, 2012).

Patty lives in Carmel Valley, California. She enjoys working out every day, cycling, scuba diving, sketching, painting, and good food and wine with family and friends. And she is regularly doing these things in Italy, except for the scuba diving (and she doesn't actually enjoy the working out).

You can find Patty online at www.PattyAzzarello.com.

INDEX